D1017434

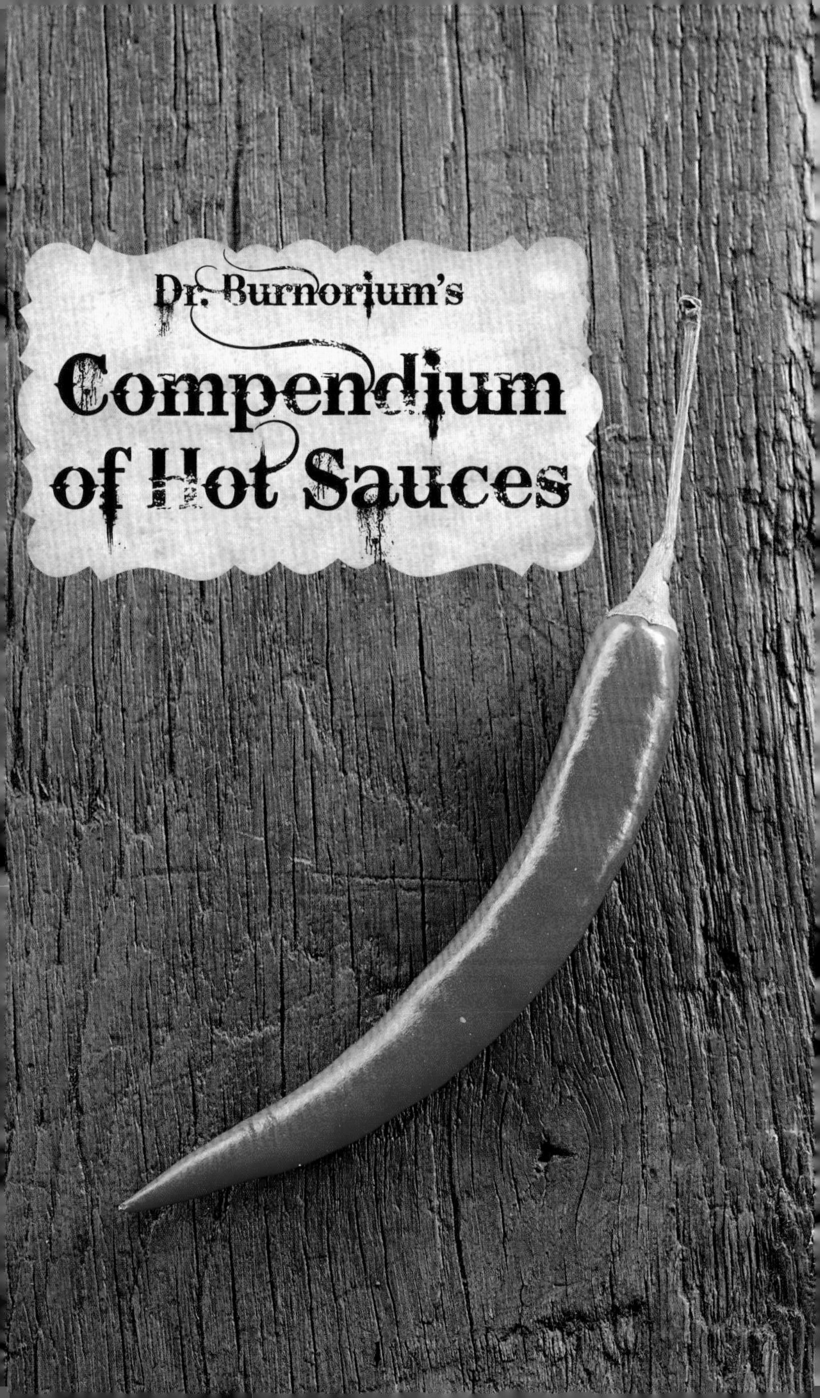
Dr. Burnorium's
Compendium
of Hot Sauces

Dr. Burnorium's Compendium of Hot Sauces

Can you handle the heat from 40 of the world's finest, face-meltingest hot sauces?

Published in 2012 by Dog 'n' Bone Books
An imprint of Ryland Peters & Small Ltd
20–21 Jockey's Fields
London WC1R 4BW
519 Broadway, 5th Floor
New York, NY 10012

www.dogandbonebooks.com

10 9 8 7 6 5 4 3 2 1

A CIP catalog record for this book is available from the Library of Congress and the British Library.

ISBN: 978 0 957140 93 6

Printed in China

Editor: Tim Leng
Design: Mark Latter
Photography: Martin Norris
Additional photography: Peter Cassidy pages 1, 2, 16, 17, 20, 102, 108, 120, 122, 125
Martin Brigdale pages 104, 107, 110, 113, 114, 117, 119
Ian Wallace page 106
Illustration: Steve Bright

For digital editions, visit www.cicobooks.com/apps.php

contents

the sauces

the recipes

Introduction

My name is Dr. Burnorium, purveyor of pain, cremator of the living, melter of faces, creator of Psycho Juice hot sauce, and proprietor of Dr. Burnorium's Hot Sauce Emporium. I invite you one and all: the chilihead, the thrill-seeker, the adventurer, the intrepid, the macho, the mischievous, the enlightened, the curious, the compulsive, the slightly nervous, and even the downright petrified, to join me as I commit my erratic ramblings to print and share with you my burning passion for all things fiery.

The following pages will take you on a journey deep into the fiery bowels of my world of hot sauce, revealing my collection of the greatest chili sauces on the planet and how they taste. I suppose it's a bit like a chilihead version of Willy Wonka's Chocolate Factory apart from the fact that my stuff doesn't rot your teeth or make you fat ... and it's hotter.

Through my website www.hotsauceemporium.co.uk and my shop in Bristol, UK, I offer an array of the world's finest fiery products to thousands of fellow chiliheads. I've personally tasted every single product I sell and I use and enjoy them on a daily basis, so whether you're a seasoned chilihead or a reluctant chili-virgin I have something for you that will blow your mind, set your taste buds alight, and banish the bland from your life forever.

So, how did this all start I hear you ask? Well, for Dr. Burnorium, it began when I was accused of being Jack the Ripper and had to flee for my life. During this time I met Salvia, an escaped freak-show dwarf whose addiction to chili led to me unlocking the secret to my immortality. But that's a story for another book.

In terms of hot sauce, things really began back in the 1860s when a man by the name of Edmund McIlhenny decided to inject some spice and fire into the bland Louisiana cuisine of the day by creating Tabasco sauce. The influence of Tabasco within the hot sauce world cannot be underestimated. It is the sauce upon which millions of us first cut our teeth and undoubtedly inspired a generation of chiliheads to start concocting their own hot sauces. It wasn't until the early 1990s that the hot sauce world as we know it today really kicked off in the USA. Not only were we offered numerous alternatives to the ubiquitous Tabasco but, with the introduction of sauces such as Blair's Death Sauces and Dave's Insanity Sauce we were also offered sauces of incredible, mind-blowing heat and these were wholeheartedly embraced by serious chiliheads. Like McIlhenny before them, both Blair (Lazar) and Dave (Hirschkop) were instrumental in pioneering a whole new market for hot sauce. Dr. Burnorium doth doff his hat.

Whilst all this was going on in the USA, a well-traveled UK businessman by the name of Cliff McAllister was exhibiting a canny eye for spotting upcoming trends. Together with his son Stuart, the McAllisters became the first people to import the likes of Dave's and Blair's sauces into the UK. The vision of this chilihead father-and-son team opened the door to a whole new hot sauce experience in the UK and for that Dr. Burnorium doth doff his hat.

Over the course of the last 20 years or so there has been a massive growth in the hot sauce market and, for many, adding fire onto or into their food has become as common as adding salt or pepper. Once you've developed a taste for chili there is no going back and, knowing that I wasn't the only one with an addiction to fiery food, I embarked upon opening the UK's first "hot shop" specializing in nothing but hot sauces and chili-related products.

There were plenty who thought I was crazy for opening such a retail outlet in the UK, but if anything that became the major driving force behind actually doing it, especially as a 'crazy' business lent itself perfectly to my somewhat unorthodox business philosophy. I don't really do "normal"—it's boring—so I adopted what I call the Motörhead approach to retail. This basically means being fucking brilliant at what you do and not giving a damn for the thoughts of those who don't get it. It's about attitude, honesty, and a total no bullshit approach. It's about separating yourself from the crowd and having the balls to be different. It's about good old-fashioned hard work, having a sense of humor, and looking after your own. It's about doing what you want to do now because you're only here once. To Lemmy, Dr. Burnorium doth doff his hat.

I can't see me being approached to write a business book based on this philosophy, although in the following pages you may well detect the influence. If you're expecting this book to be the hot sauce equivalent of some poncy wine guide, then you may well be disappointed. If you're up for a bit of a laugh and don't take things too seriously then you may well enjoy yourself.

Dr. Burnorium
Chilihead. Motörhead.
It's a way of life.

Meet the Makers

Chiliheads have a lot to be thankful for, but these four people in particular deserve the ultimate respect as over the last few decades they have helped to shape the world of hot sauce as it is today.

Blair Lazar

Back in 1989, a 19-year-old bartender by the name of Blair Lazar came up with a rather unusual way of getting the late-night drunks out of the Jersey Shore bar in which he worked. He served them chicken wings doused in his own super-hot sauce and only those who survived Blair's Wings of Death could stay past the 2am closing time. Few met the challenge because, unbeknown to them, Blair had actually been one of the first people to ever use capsaicin extract in a hot sauce. He'd noticed that the drums of pickles that they used for sandwiches in the bar contained an added ingredient—concentrated pepper extract—to make them more flavorful. The extract-makers thought he was crazy but Blair started adding this pepper extract to his wing sauce. Despite the pain it inflicted upon his drunken patrons they soon started to request the sauce for themselves. Blair's Death Sauce was born. As a true innovator with a passion for what he was doing Blair invested $550 of bartending tips and set about bottling and selling his Death Sauce.

From a small-scale outfit producing just a few cases of sauce with labels printed at his local Staples store, Blair's sauces have become nothing short of a global phenomenon with his products now being sold in more than 20 countries around the world. The most famous of these is the Blair's 16 Million Reserve which contains crystals of pure capsaicin and entered the **Guinness Book of World Records** as the hottest product ever created.

CaJohn

John Hard, otherwise known as CaJohn, has been involved in the business of "fire" for most of his life. From an early age he helped out in his father's fire protection business before becoming qualified as a Fire Protection Engineer. Ironic then that he is now best known for starting fires rather than avoiding them, producing a large range of hot sauces that have earned him in excess of 350 prestigious awards. CaJohn developed a love of heat from trips to the Caribbean, Texas, Louisiana, and the Southwest, and in 1996 he took his first steps into the fiery food world by selling the very products that he himself enjoyed. By 1999 CaJohn had begun to sell a range of his own products and within a couple of years he had opened his own manufacturing facility in Ohio. It is here that the CaJohn's legend exploded into the much-respected brand that it is today, having developed a range of some 150 products, each one manufactured in small batches with a fanatical eye for quality and flavor.

Marie Sharp

Marie Sharp is world renowned for her exceptional hot sauces. She originates from Belize, Central America, where she first came up with the idea of creating wonderful fiery concoctions for her family and friends using locally farmed Habanero peppers back in the early 1980s. The response was overwhelming and Marie decided to turn her cottage industry into a business. The key to the success of Marie's sauces, as anyone who's ever tried them will tell you, is the incredible flavor of the Habanero pepper perfectly balanced within a carrot base. Unfortunately for Marie, she suffered a major setback in the early days when her first American distributor trademarked the original name of her sauce (it wasn't called Marie Sharp's) and began to produce it as their own. With no money to fight her corner in court Marie had little option but to give up her original sauce and start again, this time using the name Marie Sharp's. This feisty and determined spirit has resulted in her wonderful sauces now being sold all over the world.

David Ashley

David Ashley is the President of the Ashley Food Company in Massachusetts, home of the infamous Mad Dog range of hot sauces, BBQ sauces, and pure capsaicin extracts. David first learned the importance of quality ingredients when he was general manager of Alice's Restaurant in Massachusetts and in 1985 he took the first tentative steps into the world that would come to regard him as a chili alchemist by producing a BBQ sauce with a kick. Fast forward five years and David was supplying his Mad Dog BBQ sauce to so many of his friends and colleagues that Mrs. Ashley took what would prove to be one of the best steps ever in the chili world. She kicked David out of the kitchen and into full-scale commercial production. On behalf of chiliheads everywhere I'd like to say "thank you" Mrs. Ashley. Like many true innovators with a burning passion for what they do, David set up the Ashley Food Company with nothing more than sheer determination, discerning taste-buds, and his credit cards. His reward has been the creation of an award-winning brand that is respected by devout chiliheads across the globe.

The Scoville Scale

Understanding Chili Heat

OK, I admit it: I'm totally addicted to hot sauces and fiery foods. I add some kind of chili to every single meal I eat. There's good reason for this, and for those of us who enjoy eating spicy foods that reason is obvious. The active component in chili peppers is a substance called capsaicin which is found predominantly in the membranes and placental tissue holding the seeds but, contrary to popular belief, not so much in the actual seeds themselves.

When consuming fiery foods, capsaicin comes into contact with the nerves in your mouth. It's an irritant and it tastes hot, so pain signals are sent to your brain. Your brain responds by releasing endorphins which are like your body's natural painkillers. These endorphins resemble opiates in the way that they produce a sense of well-being and euphoria, so, even though your mouth may be on fire, you feel good.

It is this that gives chili its addictive quality. You remember the good feeling and actively crave more of the same. Over time your tolerance to the heat builds and you turn to even hotter foods to give you the same feeling.

So, the hotter the food, the more endorphins released and the better you feel. Simple.

But how hot is hot?

In 1912 an American chemist by the name of Wilbur Scoville set about finding the answer to this question and the test he devised was known as the Scoville Organoleptic Test.

The test consisted of diluting chili pepper extract with sugar syrup until the heat was no longer detectable to a panel of tasters. The degree of dilution then gave its measure on the Scoville Scale. Therefore, a bell pepper which contains no capsaicin at all has a Scoville rating of zero.

At the other end of the scale, the Naga Jolokia (Ghost Pepper) has a rating of approximately 1 million Scovilles which means its extract has to be diluted at least a million times before the capsaicin can no longer be detected.

Good old Wilbur was undoubtedly a top bloke, but the biggest flaw in his method of testing was the fact that it relied on human subjectivity and, as we know, we're all different and what's hot to one is not necessarily so hot to another.

The scientific bit

Nowadays a method known as High Performance Liquid Chromatography (HPLC) is used to measure the pungency of peppers.

HPLC identifies and measures the heat-producing chemicals in peppers which are then bombarded with mathematical formulae containing a mind-boggling array of letters, numbers in brackets, and square root symbols; probably by some professor with a brain the size of a planet.

Personally I prefer Wilbur's method Sure it's not perfect, but the guy is a legend in the world of chili and, what's more, he didn't rely on a laboratory full of machines and a bionic version of Stephen Hawking to work out the results. He just took normal people and melted their faces off for his own ~~amusement~~ research. A man after my own heart. Fair play to you Wilbur.

PEPPERS/PRODUCT	SCOVILLE UNITS
Pure Capsaicin	16,000,000
Blair's 16 Million Reserve	16,000,000
The Source	7,100,000
US Police Pepper Spray	5,000,000
Mad Dog 357 Pepper Extract	5,000,000
Mad Dog 44 Magnum Pepper Extract	4,000,000
Mad Dog 38 Special Pepper Extract	3,000,000
Mad Dog 22 Midnight Special Pepper Extract	2,000,000
Trinidad Scorpion Butch T	1,463,700
Mad Dog's Revenge	1,000,000
Dorset Naga	923,000
Satan's Blood	800,000
Mad Dog 357 Silver Collector's Edition	750,000
Mad Dog 357 Hot Sauce	357,000
Red Savina Habanero	350,000 - 580,000
Scotch Bonnet	100,000 - 325,000
Rocoto	50,000 - 100,000
Pequin	75,000
Super Chili	40,000 - 50,000
Cayenne	30,000 - 50,000
Tabasco Pepper	30,000 - 50,000
de Arbol	15,000 - 30,000
Aji	12,000 - 30,000
Serrano	5,000 - 23,000
Hot Wax	5,000 - 10,000
Chipotle	5,000 - 10,000
Jalapeño	2,500 - 8,000
Guajillo	2,500 - 5,000
Tabasco Sauce	2,500 - 5,000
Pasilla	1,000 - 2,000
Ancho	1,000 - 2,000
Anaheim	500 - 2,500
Nu Mex	500 - 1,000
Pimento	100 - 500
Bell Pepper	0

The Axis of Evil

Here's a guide to the stars of the show, the chilis that bring the heat to hot sauces, plus a few simple recipes if you ever fancy attempting to make your own.

Naga Jolokia or Ghost Pepper

The Naga Jolokia originates from the Assam, Nagaland, and Manipur areas of Northeast India and is also known as the Bhut Jolokia, as well as the more generic term Ghost Pepper. Weighing in at over 1 million Scoville Heat Units (SHU) the Naga Jolokia entered the **Guinness Book of World Records** in 2007 as the world's hottest chili pepper. The elongated fruits have a slightly gnarled, undulating appearance, normally measure between 2–3 in. (5–7.5 cm) in length, and ripen from green through to orange to bright red. The Naga Jolokia is incredibly hot but has the most wonderful fruity flavor and aroma. It is ideal for cooking if you like your food really hot, but extreme care should be exercised when handling and cutting the fruit. The Naga Jolokia is also perfect to use in hot sauce recipes and I use the Ghost Pepper in my own Psycho Juice sauces to give blistering heat without the use of capsaicin extract.

Basic Naga Jolokia (Ghost Pepper) Hot Sauce

10 Naga Jolokia peppers, chopped
1½ cups (300 g) carrots, chopped
1 onion, chopped
4 cloves garlic, minced
½ cup (120 ml) lime juice
1 cup (240 ml) white vinegar
2 tsp salt

1. Combine all the ingredients in a saucepan, bring to the boil, and simmer for 10–15 minutes until the carrots and onions are soft. Remove from the heat and leave to cool.
2. Transfer the mixture to a food-processor and blitz the ingredients until smooth, adjusting the consistency with more vinegar if necessary. Sieve the ingredients if you want a really smooth finish.
3. Decant the sauce into a sterilized bottle or jar. It will pack some serious heat. If you don't want the sauce quite as hot, just add fewer peppers.

Habanero

Although now grown across the world, the Habanero originates from Mexico and comes in many different varieties and colors. It is one of the hottest chili peppers, measuring between 100,000 and 350,000 Scoville Heat Units (SHU). The hottest variety of Habanero is the Red Savina which measures between 350,000 and 577,000 SHU and, up until the discovery of the Naga Jolokia, was officially the hottest chili in the world. Despite its searing heat the Habanero has the most incredible fruity, tropical flavor and can be used in a whole host of culinary concoctions. Because of their amazing flavor and ability to perfectly complement other ingredients Habanero chili peppers are now used extensively in the production of hot sauces. My own Psycho Juice sauces are produced using a 70 per cent pepper content of both regular Habanero and Red Savina Habanero, which really showcases the chili pepper itself—and, believe me, when something tastes as good as the Habanero it deserves to take center stage.

Fire Roasted Habanero Hot Sauce

10 Habanero peppers, stems removed
6 plum tomatoes
1 onion, peeled and quartered
4 cloves garlic
Olive oil for drizzling
1 cup (240 ml) white vinegar
½ cup (120 ml) orange juice
2 tsp salt

1. Drizzle the Habanero peppers, tomatoes, onion, and garlic with olive oil and pan roast for about 20 minutes, turning frequently, until they take on a good color.
2. Transfer to a food-processor and add the vinegar, orange juice, and salt. Blitz until smooth and then transfer to a saucepan and simmer gently for five minutes. Adjust the consistency with water if required.
3. Allow the sauce to cool and transfer to a sterilized bottle or jar. For an extra smooth sauce, sieve before bottling.

Chipotle

The Chipotle chili originates from Mexico but can be traced back to Aztec times. It is basically a Jalapeño pepper that has been dried and wood-smoked using mesquite or sometimes pecan. Traditionally, the smoking occurred in two pits dug into the ground and connected with a tunnel. In the first pit a fire would be lit using mesquite while the peppers were placed on a rack in the second pit. The smoke would travel through the interconnecting tunnel, drying and smoking the peppers. Chipotles are between 5,000 and 10,000 Scoville Heat Units (SHU) but, although not particularly hot, their flavor is incredible with a beautiful earthy, tobacco-like smokiness. Because of the nature of production all Chipotles come in dried form and need rehydrating before they can be used. This simply involves covering the peppers with boiling water for 20–30 minutes until they soften and plump up, at which stage they can be chopped and added to your cooking.

Basic Chipotle Hot Sauce

12 Chipotle peppers, rehydrated in boiling water

1 onion, chopped

4 cloves garlic, minced

2 cups (475 ml) white vinegar

2 cups (475 ml) water (reserved from soaking the Chipotles)

½ cup (90 g) passata (sieved tomato juice)

¼ cup (60 ml) lime juice

2 tsp salt

1. Put all the ingredients in a saucepan, bring to the boil, and simmer until the sauce reduces to a desirable thickness.
2. Allow the sauce to cool, transfer to a food-processor, and blitz until smooth, adjusting the consistency with more vinegar if necessary.
3. Strain the sauce though a sieve and decant into a sterilized bottle or jar.

Trinidad Scorpion

Within the space of a few months in 2011 the chili world went a bit mad with regular new claims for the title of hottest chili in the world. The Naga Jolokia (Ghost Pepper) measured 1.1 million Scoville Heat Units (SHU), the Infinity Chili came in at 1.2 million SHU, and then the Naga Viper at 1.3 million SHU. Then along came the Trinidad Scorpion Butch T weighing in at a world record 1.4 million SHU. Although the origins of the Trinidad Scorpion pepper lie in Trinidad, the Butch T variety was actually grown in Australia. Where it will all end is anyone's guess, but one thing is certain: all of the aforementioned peppers are mind-blowingly hot with a capsaicin content beyond belief. Unless you grow your own you're going to be hard pushed to get hold of fresh Trinidad Scorpion peppers, but should you come across some I recommend you exercise caution and definitely wear gloves when handling or chopping.

Basic Trinidad Scorpion Escovitch Sauce

4 Trinidad Scorpion peppers,
sliced into thin strips *USE GLOVES*

1 onion, sliced into thin rings

10 allspice berries

½ cup (120 ml) white vinegar

½ cup (120 ml) water

1 tbsp vegetable oil

½ tbsp sugar

½ tsp salt

1. Put the ingredients in a saucepan and bring to the boil. Continue to boil for about 5 minutes.

2. Pour the sauce over your fish or chicken. WARNING—VERY HOT.

Scotch Bonnet

Few things epitomize Caribbean cuisine like the wonderful Scotch Bonnet pepper. Used extensively in traditional Jamaican jerk sauces, jerk seasonings, and escovitch sauces, the Scotch Bonnet measures between 100,000 and 350,000 Scoville Heat Units (SHU) and imparts a wonderful fiery heat with a complex fruity flavor. Although possibly originally named because of its similarity to the traditional Scottish Tam o' Shanter bonnet, the Scotch Bonnet is also known as the Goat Pepper because its odor apparently resembles that of a male goat. Having never got up-close and personal with a male goat I can neither confirm nor deny this fact. One thing is for certain: they taste fantastic, and although not used as widely as Habanero in the production of hot sauces outside of the Caribbean, there are some amazing Scotch Bonnet products about.

Basic Caribbean-Style Scotch Bonnet Hot Sauce

12 Scotch Bonnet peppers, chopped
2 onions, chopped
4 cloves garlic, chopped
1 papaya, chopped
½ cup (120 ml) lime juice
1½ cups (350 ml) white vinegar
½ cup (125 g) yellow mustard
2 tsp salt
2 tsp curry powder (optional)

1. Put the chopped Scotch Bonnet peppers, onions, garlic, papaya, and lime juice into a food-processor and blitz until smooth. You may have to do this in batches.
2. Put the puréed ingredients into a saucepan and stir in the vinegar, mustard, salt, and curry powder if using. Simmer the purée over a gentle heat, stirring occasionally, for about 20 minutes, adjusting the consistency with more vinegar if necessary.
3. Allow to cool and decant into a sterilized bottle or jar. If you want a really smooth sauce, then sieve before bottling.

Cayenne

The Cayenne pepper has been used for centuries for both its culinary and medicinal qualities. This fiery chili measures between 30,000 and 50,000 Scoville Heat Units (SHU), and is usually dried and powdered or processed for use within the production of Louisiana-style hot sauces. Although originating from French Guiana, Cayenne is now grown in many countries across the world, with the USA accounting for the vast majority of its production. Reputedly used extensively in the ancient Mayan and Aztec cultures, the Cayenne pepper was highly prized for its ability to combat, amongst other things, toothache and scabies. The Cayenne pepper has a sweetish, slightly bitter taste and packs a good punch of heat that's guaranteed to spice up any dish. Unless you grow your own, the chances are you will only be able to get Cayenne in dried form, in which case you'll need to rehydrate the peppers in boiling water for 20–30 minutes until they soften.

Basic Louisiana-Style Hot Sauce

1lb (450 g) Cayenne peppers, chopped
2 cups (475 ml) white vinegar
2 tsp salt

1. Put the ingredients in a saucepan, bring to the boil, and simmer for 10 minutes.
2. Allow to cool, transfer to a food-processor, and blitz the ingredients until smooth.
3. Decant the sauce into a sterilized jar and put the jar in the fridge, leaving it in there to mature for a few weeks.
4. Before use, strain the sauce through a sieve and adjust consistency with more vinegar if necessary.

Confessions of a Chili Masochist

Few things in life are more enjoyable than witnessing the agony of someone who's taken it upon themselves to sample some of the super-hot sauces that I sell. Tough guys, macho men, cocky gobshites, they've all beaten a hasty retreat from my shop with faces as red as a baboon's ass and a willingness to sell their backside for a glass of milk. If you've ever wondered what it feels like to eat such a sauce, there's one guy who knows only too well, Leo Scott. For the last few years he's been testing many of the sauces featured in the book and you can see the results at www.youtube.com/user/HomeGrownUkChili. Here's a few words from the man himself on feeling the burn.

Dr. Burnorium So, Leo, why did you start consuming the hot stuff, filming the results, and posting them on YouTube?
Leo Well, as a self-confessed masochist I loved watching people on YouTube eat stupidly hot products and chilies and of course suffering as a result, so, I thought, "Hell yeah—I'll have a go at that!" Tried it, loved it, had a good audience response, so from that day forward I haven't looked back; still reviewing, still suffering, and on a partial diet of anti-indigestion tablets.

Dr. Burnorium So it was nothing to do with the fact that I caught you shoplifting in my place, stuck you down the cellar, forced you to inflict pain upon yourself, and put the videos on YouTube?
Leo Are you crazy or something?!? I've never shoplifted from your place… Cellar… What cellar?? You lured me into this burning situation by introducing me to Blair's Ultra Death and destroying my taste buds. I seem to need more and more heat just to taste anything these days. It's all your fault!

Dr. Burnorium Yes, I remember the Blair's Ultra Death video. A full tablespoon and report to camera. It looked like you were in serious pain. Did it hurt?
Leo Did it hurt? What kind of question is that?! It had some flavor, but then: POW! Felt like a big chili fist knocked me to the floor. My tongue and throat felt like I had just swallowed napalm. I couldn't taste anything for hours after, and it felt like crapping Satan's breath itself the next morning.

Dr. Burnorium Quite painful then. That's what you get for shoplifting. What was the response like to the YouTube video?
Leo It was painful for sure! People were amazed I consumed so much. They also seem to enjoy watching me in pain, too. Basically they said, "We want more!" "You have the funniest 'pain-face,'" and "Why do that to yourself?" Well, I say, I'm a little crazy and love to feel the burn… Bring it on!!

Dr. Burnorium And bring it on you did. You've since gone on to do YouTube videos of nearly every ultra-hot sauce I sell. Did you pay for those?
Leo I paid for the first sauce, then when I returned you just said, "You're a nut-case! Fancy reviewing this? You won't have to pay for it…" Dr. Burnorium then hands over a bottle of Mad Dog 357 Silver Collector's Edition, the hottest sauce available on the market commercially, and says, "If you're able to handle that, do you want to do more reviews with sauces?" I was a little skeptical but agreed…

Dr. Burnorium The Mad Dog 357 Silver Collector's Edition has brought many a grown man to his knees. Can you describe how it felt taking a full tablespoon of this stuff?
Leo Firstly, it was one of the worst experiences I've been through with reviewing sauces. That stuff is just insane. As soon as I swallowed it, it felt like the gates of hell had opened up in my stomach and started to eat me alive from the inside out. Halfway through the review my body agreed that I shouldn't have done that, and the next thing I know I was being sick and bringing it back up. That was painful, too—felt like I had been attacked with military grade pepper spray. Will never do that one again!

Dr. Burnorium That one must have put you off shoplifting for life. But then you decided to up the ante and informed me that you wanted to review The Source—7.1 Million Scovilles of pure capsaicin extract. Are you crazy? Why did you do it and what did it do to you?
Leo Crazy is as crazy does, and plus I had several thousand people over the years I've been on YouTube requesting I review The Source, so, in the end I accepted the challenge. Basically we had a large drop on a spoon and I licked it clean. I even had to break out the milk but, of course, that had no effect on me whatsoever and I had to endure the burn and pain for near enough half an hour. Pure hell.

the Sauces

Psycho Juice 70% Ghost Pepper

PERSONALITY:
Menacing, sinister

BALANCE:
Poised, elegant

BODY:
Full, muscular

BOUQUET:
Fruity, tangy

LENGTH:
Well endowed, good girth

BURN RATING

☠☠☠☠☠

The Story

Hallowe'en used to be about ghosts. Loveable street urchins dressed in white bed sheets going "woooh." How things have changed. Now you get obnoxious, monosyllabic spunk-bubbles strutting around like Freddy Krueger causing elderly folk to soil their pants as they extort chocolate out of them under the thinly veiled guise of Trick or Treat. Refusal to participate in the confectionary scam traditionally results in a "trick." This used to be nothing more sinister than having an egg chucked at your window as Casper the Friendly Ghost legged it down the road, tripping over his bed sheet as he went. Just try giving one of these Freddy fuckers the knock-back today. You'll find your garden shed on fire, the tyres slashed on your Nissan, and dog shit shoved through your letterbox.

My solution to this problem comes courtesy of my own Psycho Juice. Simply inject the sauce into any soft-centered chocolate and wait for Freddy to knock at the door. One bite and he'll be off across the road quicker than an amphetamine-fueled proton blasting down that Hadron Collider thingy. He won't even notice the oncoming traffic until the point of impact. Who's soiled their pants now Freddy?

Flavor notes:

Serious Naga Jolokia (Ghost Pepper) heat slashing through a shower curtain of carrot, onion, garlic, and lemon juice. A massive 70% pepper content gives incredible flavor, searing firepower, and all the attitude you'd expect from Dr. Burnorium. Shut up with your whinging and take your medicine. Hallowed be thy pain.

Professor Phardtpounder's Colon Cleaner

The Story

For most of us, the colon is just part of the body's shit-processing factory. To Professor Phardtpounder, however, it was an organ of wondrous beauty, albeit with an inherent problem that required some serious probing. Phardtpounder's mission was to find a way of getting fecal matter to travel through the factory in a more sprightly fashion and therefore avoid the issue of "clagging," an unfortunate business that resulted in an altogether filthy and putrid colon.

Phardtpounder found the solution to his colonic conundrum during a visit to the Caribbean where he had a brief dalliance with a lady of fulsome, homely bosom, and thighs capable of pulverizing a melon. What she also had in abundance was fiery chili peppers with which she laced everything she cooked. After a few days of fulsome homeliness, pulverization, and fiery fodder, Phardtpounder noticed that his daily evacuation process had sped up considerably. The solution had been found and Phardtpounder was in no doubt that his colon was now so clean you could eat your dinner from it.

PERSONALITY:
Lively,
feisty

BALANCE:
Graceful,
symmetrical

BODY:
Medium,
trim

BOUQUET:
Mustardy,
tangy

LENGTH:
Respectable,
satisfying

Flavor notes:

Delicious mustard background with Habanero fire. A touch of sweetness and a smidgen of turmeric give a subtle, piccalilli-like quality. Those whose senses are less defined than mine won't be able to detect gossamer back-notes of juicy melon pulverized between hefty thighs, but that's why I've been asked to write this book and they haven't.

Day of the Dead
(Dia De Los Muertos)

PERSONALITY:
Lively, feisty

BALANCE:
Poised, elegant

BODY:
Thin, loose

BOUQUET:
Smoky, spicy

LENGTH:
Respectable, satisfying

BURN RATING

💀💀💀

The Story

The Day of the Dead is an ancient festival held every year in Mexico to celebrate dead people. Whether you've passed away peacefully with your loving family at your bedside or are one of the 40,000 (and rising) who've fallen victim to Mexico's drug cartels and found yourself beheaded or hung from a bridge, you can rest safe in the knowledge that you won't be forgotten. Each year your loved ones will assemble en masse at your graveside and build you a beautiful altar festooned with orange marigolds (the flowers, not the rubber gloves), intricately decorated sugar skulls, heartfelt poems, and a selection of your favorite food and drink.

Unfortunately, attempts to recreate this fine celebration in other parts of the world have fallen somewhat short and resulted in graveyards being desecrated with altars fashioned from upturned dumpsters laden with crates of beer, packs of cigarettes, and doner kebabs with everything, no salad, and extra meat. There have been some heartfelt poems though:

I miss you Dad I want you back, why did you have a heart attack?
I've loved you since I was a foetus, I hope I don't get your diabetes.

Very moving.

Flavor notes:

The Habanero peppers probably aren't smoked with the burning wood of a freshly cremated coffin, but their wonderful earthy smokiness imparts a flavor to die for. Subtle apparitions of purééd carrot and lime dance hand-in-hand with vibrant spices and a celebratory shot of Tequila. A festival of fantastic flavor.

Mad Dog 357 Silver Collector's Edition

PERSONALITY:
Psychopathic, sadistic

BALANCE:
Taut, rigid

BODY:
Medium, trim

BOUQUET:
Spicy, death

LENGTH:
Hung like a donkey

BURN RATING

The Story

Please don't be fooled by the cutesy Simpson-esque pooch on the label. Lurking behind that butter-wouldn't-melt grin is the canine equivalent of Vlad The Impaler, armed with a flamethrower that's cocked and ready to melt your face off. This is the dog for whom the "mad or bad" debate—normally reserved for serial killers with a penchant for fashioning lamp shades from the skin of their victims—was first voiced.

The ballistically aware among you will notice that there's a bullet attached to the bottle. Unfortunately it's not a live round with which you can blow your brains out to escape the agony of this crazy concoction. The bullet, unlike the sauce, is actually harmless and unscrews to reveal a tiny tasting spoon that looks suspiciously like a spoon you might find in Tony Montana's kitchen. Please do not be a proper Charlie and use it as such. Your desire for 15 minutes of YouTube fame may well be overwhelming, but snorting this stuff will cause your nose and brain to spontaneously combust into a lava-like gloop that will spew forth from the hole where your face used to be before slopping into your lap and dissolving your genitals. Not that you'll be needing them with a face like that.

Flavor notes:

You don't so much taste this stuff as experience it. Like sticking your face into a roaring fire, removing a white-hot coal with your mouth, chewing it to dust and swallowing it. A blistering ensemble with back-notes of molten enamel, liquefied skin, and scorched facial hair. Use as a cooking additive only.

Pain is Good Jamaican

PERSONALITY:
Serious, forceful

BALANCE:
Graceful, elegant

BODY:
Full, muscular

BOUQUET:
Fruity, spicy

LENGTH:
Well endowed, good girth

BURN RATING

The Story

There is a very rare medical condition called Paralyzed Expressive Neuron Inhibiting Syndrome. PENIS for short. It's easier to get your mouth around. Triggered by an acute reaction to the heat of chili peppers, a PENIS attack leaves the victim with a pained expression permanently rogered into their face. One such sufferer is a Jamaican guy by the name of Buckwheat whose PENIS is extreme. Many sufferers are so embarrassed by their PENIS that they spend their lives locked away in a cupboard, but Buckwheat chose to let the whole world see his PENIS when he became one of the faces fronting the Pain Is Good range of hot sauces.

Buckwheat's PENIS touched me and I've now set up a charitable organization to raise money for research into this terrible condition. I've approached a collection of world leaders to front an ad campaign. "Think Politicians, Think PENIS." Works for me. I've not heard back from them yet, but in the meantime all donations can be sent to me c/o Dog 'n' Bone Books. Naturally there will be one-or-two "administration" expenses because charities don't run themselves. Please give generously and together we can help Buckwheat beat his PENIS.

Flavor notes:

Fiery Habanero fruitiness within a rich base of tomato, garlic, and jerk seasoning. Zesty lime and lemon acidity with a tad of pineapple sweetness that will waft you away on a ganja cloud to a place where pain has never tasted so good.

The Hottest Fuckin' Sauce

PERSONALITY:
Evil, dangerous

BALANCE:
Taut, rigid

BODY:
Medium, trim

BOUQUET:
Tangy, death

LENGTH:
Hung like a donkey

BURN RATING

💀💀💀💀💀💀

The Story

The Gospel According to the Sanctimonious states that using the f-word demonstrates a lack of vocabulary, intellectual laziness, and poor breeding. What a load of old crap. A carefully chosen expletive can breathe life, emphasis, and passion into a sentence that is otherwise about as riveting as the notoriously dull former UK Prime Minister John Major addressing a biscuit collector's convention. Mind you, he did become a tad more interesting once we found out he'd been shagging his colleague Edwina Currie. There. Point made. A fuck makes stuff more interesting. I rest my case.

Personally, I think more products should follow the lead of this pioneering hot sauce. I've therefore set up "BRANDFUCKER," an agency specializing in expletive-led branding—"we'll take your brand and fuck it." I've pitched the idea to a few big companies and am waiting to hear back. Could be a winner I reckon. BAKED FUCKIN' BEANS will get blokes cooking more. CARPET FUCKIN' CLEANER will lead to such an increase in male vacuuming that we'll see the introduction of the SUCKER FUCKER, a jet black model complete with a nifty can-holder for your beer and a special nozzle just for the boys. I'm sure the Language Nazis will have something to say about it, but to be honest I don't give a flying...

Flavor notes:

Not quite THE hottest, but definitely enough firepower to leave you cursing. An uncompromising, foul-mouthed blend of Habanero, Scotch Bonnet, onion, and African oleoresin. What it lacks in refinement and elegance it more than makes up for in attitude and power. Use as a cooking additive only.

Rectum Ripper

The Story

Despite the name, the Rectum Ripper is not actually a serial killer who murders his victims through their back passage. That's no doubt a disappointment for the newspapers who love nothing more than a good serial killer to help boost sales. Unfortunately for them, very few of us actually succumb to the voices in our head urging us to slip into our dead mother's underwear and go on a mass killing spree. Those who do, however, are rewarded by the newspapers with a headline-grabbing name like Slasher or Ripper.

The downside to this is when a socially inadequate 40-year-old virgin who still lives at home with his mother suddenly finds himself reborn as the read-all-about-it, shit-your-pants, modern-day Jack the Ripper. In his mangled brain he suddenly becomes a somebody. He's got a reputation to maintain. So off he pops with a hard-on to buy a new Ripper-headline-making claw hammer. The papers should actually use their power to humiliate such people. It would prevent further bloodshed. This contemporary Ripper might not have been so eager to continue his murderous campaign if he knew that he would forever be known as the Boston Ball-Bag or the Yorkshire Cock-Sucker.

PERSONALITY:
Lively,
feisty

BALANCE:
Graceful,
orderly

BODY:
Medium,
trim

BOUQUET:
Tangy,
mustardy

LENGTH:
Respectable,
satisfying

Flavor notes:

Fiery Habanero peppers ripping through a blend of crushed tomatoes, carrot, onion, and mustard. Delightful cloaked background of ginger, garlic, and lime. Decent firepower, but not the sort of heat that will leave your rectum in tatters.

West African Voodoo Juice

PERSONALITY:
Vengeful, evil

BALANCE:
Poised, elegant

BODY:
Medium, trim

BOUQUET:
Fruity, tangy, sweet

LENGTH:
Eye watering

BURN RATING

The Story

CENSORED

* Unfortunately this page has been canceled due to unacceptable, humorless, and over-sensitive editing by the publishers. If you would like to read the unedited version please email me at doctor@hotsauceemporium.co.uk and I will send you a copy. My sincere apologies for any inconvenience caused. Normal service will be resume on the following page.
Dr. Burnorium

Flavor notes:

A bubbling cauldron of Red Savina Habanero, carrot, and onion with a blend of fruity papaya, pineapple, and banana. A tad of zesty lime and a shot of brown rum complete the spell before a blast of capsaicin extract takes the whole magical concoction to the dark side. Use as a cooking additive only.

Iguana Radioactive

PERSONALITY:
Lively, feisty

BALANCE:
Poised, orderly

BODY:
Full, muscular

BOUQUET:
Fruity, tangy

LENGTH:
Respectable, satisfying

BURN RATING

💀💀💀

The Story

Unless you're a City banker who's so bloated with bonuses that you shit cash, you're probably just a lowlife peasant watching every penny. That's why multi-purpose products such as Iguana represent excellent value for money. On the one hand, you get yourself a really tasty hot sauce that will improve the flavor of the reconstituted scrotum burgers that you eat every day. On the other hand, it'll stop your snot-encrusted offspring from continually banging-on about getting a pet.

Simply take an old cardboard box you've got lying about and cut the front off. Place your bottle of sauce inside with the label facing outward. Voilà. Instant iguana and vivarium. Cheap to keep, no mess to clean up, and none of this taking-for-a-walk crap like the dog they wanted. To further enhance the exotic pet experience, you can easily recreate an iguana's natural habitat by adding a brick and some weeds from your garden. Your kids will be so fascinated by their new reptilian friend that they won't even notice you've pawned their Xbox for booze, but, best of all, once you've got the brats to bed you can bang your missus on the living room floor without fear of your iguana wandering over and sticking its nose up your chocolate starfish.

Flavor notes:

A decent fiery glow from a combination of Habanero, Cayenne, and Tabasco peppers with a full-bodied background of carrot, onion, garlic, and tomato finished with a lime zestiness and a pronounced salty edge.

Rectal Rocket Fuel

PERSONALITY:
Serious, forceful

BALANCE:
Graceful, elegant

BODY:
Medium, trim

BOUQUET:
Spicy, smoky

LENGTH:
Well endowed, good girth

BURN RATING
☠☠☠☠

The Story

LSD became popular in the early sixties and there are still a few acid casualties who insist that they were the first people in space. There was a dog, too, but it's not clear if he'd also taken LSD. The official records show that it was actually Russian cosmonaut Yuri Gagarin, aided by a spacecraft rather than mind-bending drugs, who was the first man to orbit the earth. What the records don't show, however, is that Gagarin's rocket was powered by human gas.

The Russians are renowned for their fondness of cabbage, a particularly gaseous vegetable that causes uncontrollable farting. It was discovered that by mixing cabbage with chili peppers the resulting emissions were so powerful they could probably blast a man into space. Hundreds of Russians volunteered at gunpoint to be imprisoned in a huge rocket hangar and live entirely on a diet of cabbage and chili whilst having their fiery flatulence pumped directly into the spacecraft's enormous fuel tank. On April 12, 1961 the tank was full and the countdown began. A guy called Hugo Blastov opened the valve on the fuel tank and struck a match. The launch was a spectacular success and, a bit like comrade Blastov, the rest is history.

Flavor notes:

A rocket full of wonderful jerk spices fueled by powerful Habanero and Scotch Bonnet peppers. A multi-layered launch pad of sage, thyme, garlic, paprika, and allspice fused with cumin, fennel, lemon pepper, ground coriander, and a squirt of lime. Bon voyage.

Z
Nothing Beyond

The Story

A is for ATTENTION, listen up my dears, **B is for BEWARE**, this could end in tears, **C is for CAUTION**, you need just a touch, **D is for DUMBASS**, that's way too much, **E is for ERUPTION**, of volcanic proportion, **F is for FUCKWIT**, I did advise caution, **G is for GAZE**, like a mental case, **H is for HORROR**, the look on your face, **I is for IDIOT**, you're certainly a fool, **J is for JUMPING**, around like a tool, **K is for KISSING**, the bowels of hell, **L is for LICKING**, the sun as well, **M is for MOLTEN**, the lava within, **N is for NAPALM**, running down your chin, **O is for OBLITERATED** vocal chords, **P is for PARAMEDICS** and hospital wards, **Q is for QUICK**, their help you require, **R is for RAVAGED** by internal fire, **S is for SCREAM**, your last desperate plea, **T is for TORTURED** to the nth degree, **U is for UNIT**, specializing in pain, **V is for VIOLENT** shocks through your brain, **W is for WORRY**, this cannot be solved, **X is for X-RAY**, your bones have dissolved, **Y is for YOU**, deceased, can't respond, **Z is for Z, and there's NOTHING BEYOND**.

BURN RATING

PERSONALITY:
Crazy,
dangerous

BALANCE
Elegant,
rigid

BODY:
Medium,
trim

BOUQUET:
Fruity,
tangy

LENGTH:
Hung like
a donkey

Flavor notes:

Tangy mustard and tomato base combined with exotic papaya, guava, pineapple, banana, and passion fruit. A veritable fruity forest fire that's well and truly ablaze with scorching Habanero and capsaicin extract. You won't be putting this one out in a hurry. Use as a cooking additive only.

Blair's After Death

PERSONALITY:
Dangerous, murderous

BALANCE:
Rigid, poised

BODY:
Medium, trim

BOUQUET:
Tangy, fruity

LENGTH:
Eye watering

BURN RATING

The Story

Body disposal is the bane of a murderer's life. Traditionally, corpses have just been dumped in ditches or left in the woods for dog-walkers to find, but with today's advances in forensic techniques you'd have to be an absolute lunatic to offload a body in such an amateurish fashion. Leave so much as a stray hair in the throat of your victim and some boffin will perform all manner of scientific jiggery-pokery to extract your DNA—the magical code that discloses your name, address, and telephone number to the police. Basically, you're well and truly rumbled pal.

Although not originally designed for the purpose, the appropriately named After Death has proved a highly effective method of dissolving troublesome corpses. Simply place the body in an empty bathtub and douse liberally with After Death. Leave for 24 hours and abracadabra, liquid cadaver. Just turn on the taps and rinse the slurry straight down the plughole. No mess, no pubes, no evidence. As an added bonus, After Death comes complete with a skull keyring. This beautifully crafted plastic skull is the perfect murder memento and, should you go on to do further killings, they can be used as a handy way of keeping a tally on the body-count.

Flavor notes:

A deathly combination of Habanero, Cayenne, and Chipotle peppers cranked up by more than a few notches with the addition of capsaicin extract. A solid hit of smashed garlic is complemented by a subtle spicy smokiness. Much better on food than corpses.

The Story

I was in the shop filling my shelves with Wet Fart the other day and found myself reminiscing about childish humor. Remember those good old-fashioned joke shops? A veritable Aladdin's cave of practical jokes, magic tricks, and general tomfoolery... Whatever happened to them and the shady, over-friendly guy behind the counter? I reckon it's an institution that needs reviving. Obviously, kids of today have become acclimatized to blood and gore through blasting the face off anything that moves on their Xbox, so practical jokes would need to be updated accordingly.

The hilarious "mousetrap chewing gum" that nips your finger when you remove a stick of gum from the packet needs beefing-up with a spring that's so powerful it'll take your thumb off. And instead of chewing gum it could be a joint. The classic plastic "bloody finger" should be a real bloody finger that's been hacked from a sex-offender using a blunt, rusty machete. And, while they are at it, they can remove his eyeballs with a spoon and stick them to the springs that are fixed to a pair of those goofy plastic specs. The side-splitting "whoopee cushion" was always my favorite. This needs to be filled with the foul liquid waste of an alcoholic tramp who feeds from the bins at the back of an Indian restaurant and it should be made from balloon-like material that bursts when someone sits on it. The ultimate wet fart. Oh how they'll laugh.

PERSONALITY:
Lively,
feisty

BALANCE:
Elegant,
orderly

BODY:
Trim,
muscular

BOUQUET:
Tangy,
fruity,
spicy

LENGTH:
Respectable,
satisfying

Flavor notes:

Don't be put off by the name, this sauce is definitely no joke when it comes to flavor. Habanero and aged red peppers tempered by a sublime blend of Parmesan and romano cheese. A solid background of carrots, onion, garlic, and tomato complemented with a tad of honey sweetness and zippy lime.

One Fuckin' Drop at a Time

PERSONALITY:
Evil, dangerous

BALANCE:
Taut, rigid

BODY:
Thin, loose

BOUQUET:
Tangy, death

LENGTH:
Hung like a donkey

BURN RATING

💀💀💀💀💀💀

The Story

After receiving the following correspondence, this page has been postponed whilst I seek advice from Salman Rushdie.

Dear Dr. Burnorium,
Having just read The Hottest F***in' Sauce on page 32. I don't mind telling you that I was shocked to the point of apoplexy. Never have I seen such disgusting language committed to print. The constant barrage of f-words was intolerable. Effing this, effing that, and effing the other. I just hope you're proud of the fact that you effed me until I very nearly fainted. You scatter profanities like confetti at the wedding I never had. Well, let me tell you something Burnorium, God is my companion and I can assure you that, after a hard day at work, He doesn't come home and enter through the back door whilst using foul and abusive language. It makes you no less the devil incarnate that just about the only profanity you don't ejaculate from your satanic organ is the word c***. I've passed your book of Beelzebub onto my local priest and I feel it only fair to warn you that he has friends in high places– and I don't just mean the police who helped to get him off the slanderous charges from the local scout troop. I will not waste my breath praying for you Burnorium. I hope you get everything that's coming your way and more. Cross my path at your peril. I've got a crucifix and I'm not scared to use it. **Watch your effing back.**

Flavor notes:

Comes with a handy pipette dropper with which to cautiously despatch this crazy concoction of blisteringly hot Habanero, Scotch Bonnet, and African oleoresin. Don't be a dumbass and blast this all over your pizza. Use as a cooking additive only.

Psycho Juice 70% Red Savina

The Story

You may think that the life of a successful entrepreneur and multi-award-winning author is a never-ending maelstrom of unimaginable wealth, sexy ladies who'll go to bed with you at the drop of a hat, and hero-worship from an army of adoring fans. And, of course, you'd be right. Occasionally, however, even someone as brilliant as me can attract a bit of negative feedback (check out the mad woman on page 49). Thankfully, most of the letters I receive are from normal people rather than weirdos. Like this one from a fan who wrote to me from Broadmoor Psychiatric Hospital. Probably a fellow doctor or a brain surgeon or something.

Dear Dr. Burnorium, My mom visit and bring Psycho Juice. I like juice. I don't like the voices. I don't like Barry. He take Psycho Juice. I fight Barry and bottle break. I angry. Voices say do things. I hostage Barry. Barry boohoo. Wardens bang cell door. I hit broken bottle on Barry. Barry not boohoo now. I cut Barry's ear off. I dip in Juice. Tastes nice. Think I here for longer now. Please send more Psycho Juice. In plastic bottle. I not allowed glass now. I think

(At this point the text becomes difficult to read, but the letter appears to continue):

you are absolutely brilliant and Psycho Juice is without doubt the finest hot sauce ever. Anyone who ever criticizes you is clearly mentally ill and doesn't know what they're on about. If I ever hear of anyone doing such a thing I'll cut their ear off. Keep up the good work and I hope you win loads of awards for your book, your sauces, and for being an amazing person. PS. You're the best. Seriously, you're great.

PERSONALITY:
Serious,
forceful

BALANCE:
Poised,
elegant

BODY:
Full,
muscular

BOUQUET:
Fruity,
tangy

LENGTH:
Well endowed,
good girth

BURN RATING

💀💀💀💀

Flavor notes:

Parp! Parp! I'm not one to blow my own trumpet but this is probably one of the finest hot sauces you'll ever taste. The wonderful, fruity, fiery Red Savina Habanero is the star of the show and accompanied to perfection by a blend of carrot, onion, garlic, and zesty lemon. Parp! Parp!

Mad Dog's Revenge

PERSONALITY:
Psychopathic, deadly

BALANCE:
Totally unhinged

BODY:
Thin

BOUQUET:
Funeral wreath

LENGTH:
Never ending

Flavor notes:

Forget it. Just use literally a drop at a time in your cooking.

BURN RATING

The Story

With his trademark yellow complexion, chef's hat, and cheeky grin, Mad Dog is one of the most famous faces in the hot-sauce world. Behind that grin, however, is a story of pain and a thirst for revenge. In his new autobiography **Mad Dog: Cross Me and I'll Take Your Face Off** he tells of the events that led to his descent into revenge-fueled madness. Now, in an exclusive deal with yours truly, you can read a series of extracts from his book for the first time.

"My problems started back in the early sixties when I was sacked as drummer of The Beatles and replaced by that bastard Ringo Starr. Lennon, McCartney, and the other one hadn't even got the balls to tell me to my face and left it to Brian Epstein to do their dirty work. He told me that my drumming wasn't up to scratch, but I knew the real reason. Racism. It's because I was yellow. If there's one thing I hate it's prejudice and discrimination, especially from a sausage-jockey. I just lost it and started growling and snarling and snapping as I chased The Beatles around Abbey Road Studios. The next thing I know I'm waking up in hospital. The doctor told me I'd got serious problems. Damn right I had. I'd just been sacked by The Beatles and I'd left my notebook behind with all my songs in it. He suggested I see a psychiatrist but I didn't need someone who could see into the future to tell me that all the songs I'd written for the as yet unreleased albums such as **Rubber Soul**, **Sgt. Pepper's Lonely Hearts Club Band**, and the **White Album** would earn The Beatles millions. These were dark days indeed, and I did start to drink. Mainly in East London's Blind Beggar pub, where I became really good friends with notorious local gangsters, the Kray Twins. I was sat drinking in the Blind Beggar with Ron and Reg one day when the fat, mental one (can never remember which is which) offered to murder The Beatles for me. He even showed me how he'd do it by shooting a guy at the bar in the face. I appreciated the offer, but I knew that the best way to get my revenge was to become more successful than The Beatles. I bid the Kray Twins farewell and bought a one-way ticket to the US of A. I was going to be a movie star." Continues on page 87.

Marie Sharp's Green Habanero

PERSONALITY:
Lively, feisty

BALANCE:
Poised, elegant

BODY:
Medium, trim

BOUQUET:
Fruity, citrusy

LENGTH:
Reasonable, satisfying

BURN RATING

💀💀💀

The Story

A cactus is basically a large penis-shaped plant covered in loads of really sharp prickles so you've got to question the sanity of the person who first thought it looked good enough to eat. Whoever it was, we've ultimately got them to thank for this wonderful cactus-based hot sauce. It's actually made with nopal, or prickly pear, which rather than being a phallic cactus is more reminiscent of a lady's vagina minus the beef-curtains. And with prickles instead of pubes. Google it if you don't believe me. Although common in Mexican cuisine the only time nopal was ever used in the UK was in Nopal Fruits, the delicious, chewy fruit sweets that were "made to make your mouth water." Unfortunately, due to a manufacturing problem with the de-prickling machine, they had to remove the cactus-flavored sweets because not only did they "make your mouth water," but they also made your throat spew blood when the prickles punctured your windpipe. Rumor has it that Nopal Fruits were rebranded as Starburst shortly after a prickle nearly killed the Queen Mother. This was alledgedly covered up at the time and blamed on a fish bone because the royal family didn't want to risk headline-writers saying that the Queen Mother had nearly choked to death when she got a prick stuck in her throat.

Flavor notes:

Outstanding hot sauce with a sophisticated base of nopal/prickly pear cactus puncturing the fiery heat of fruity green Habanero peppers. There is a perfect balance from the onion and garlic which give way to an incredible citrusy lime finish. Absolutely beautiful and guaranteed prickle-free.

Blair's Ultra Death

PERSONALITY:
Evil,
dangerous

BALANCE:
Poised,
orderly

BODY:
Trim,
muscular

BOUQUET:
Tangy,
fruity

LENGTH:
Hung like
a donkey

BURN RATING

The Story

Blair's After Death (see page 44) revolutionized the way that murderers dispose of their victims. Although highly effective, the one downside to After Death is that it takes 24 hours to dissolve a corpse. Sometimes it's simply not practical to have a body lying around in your bathtub for so long. Maybe you've done your missus in whilst the kids are downstairs eating their dinner and you need to get her swilled away before their bath time. You'll be doing the school run now, so you want them looking neat and tidy. Or maybe you're the next Jeffrey Dahmer and you wake up each morning to find another corpse in your festering apartment. Sure the company is nice but frankly the stench is becoming unbearable. Not only that, you've run out of seating and you can't even answer the door without tripping over various body parts.

Whatever, if you need to get rid of a corpse in double-quick time Ultra Death is the answer. This stuff is so powerful it dissolves on contact. No more waiting. A nice touch with Ultra Death is that it comes in a beautiful, coffin-shaped box that is ideal for storing a "trophy" from your victim. There's plenty of room for a pair of knickers, a finger, or even a couple of nipples and some pubic shavings. Murder memories that you can treasure.

Flavor notes:

A mind-blowing concoction of Habanero, Serrano, and Naga Jolokia peppers enhanced to murderous levels with capsaicin extract. Definitely a cooking additive rather than a marinade for your favorite cut of meat.

Acid Rain

The Story

Scientists around the world now agree that Acid Rain was not caused by pollution as initially thought. In an ironic twist of fate, research shows that it was actually caused by hippies. Back in the sixties, long-haired beatniks were turning on, tuning in, and dropping out with LSD. This psychedelic drug, also known as Acid, took the user on a mind-bending "trip" that enabled them to talk to unicorns, watch their fingers turn into snakes, and fly from high-rise buildings like Superman. This didn't go down well with the authorities who wanted Acid to be used for responsible things like mind control and chemical warfare. They told the hippies to fuck off and banned it.

Undeterred, the hippies continued to make Acid in their bathtubs. Not only was it exceptionally clean because the bath had never been used, but it also meant that if there was a police raid they could get rid of any incriminating evidence by simply pulling the plug. Over the years millions of gallons of Acid have been disposed of in such a manner. Unfortunately for the environment the psychoactive substance had to go somewhere and, over the course of time, most of it ended up in the atmosphere and formed into clouds. Although Acid Clouds look like normal clouds—apart from the fact they're shaped like smiley faces and have a tie-dye pattern—the Acid Rain that they produce can have a devastating effect. A dose from a single cloud can cause buildings to crumble and dissolve before your very eyes; unicorn forests to wither and die; and lakes to suddenly bubble with the blood of a million dead fish that float upon its surface. A bit like a bad Acid trip really. So there you have it. Hippies screwed the planet.

PERSONALITY:
Lively,
feisty

BALANCE:
Poised,
elegant

BODY:
Medium,
trim

BOUQUET:
Fruity,
tangy

LENGTH:
Reasonable,
satisfying

BURN RATING

Flavor notes:

A veritable cloudburst of chili heat and flavor from a blend of Habanero, Piquin, Tepin, Ring of Fire, Peri-peri, and Jalapeño peppers. A well-balanced climate of spices, garlic, and ginger complemented with a light drizzle of lemon, lime, and orange. Let it rain, let it rain, let it rain.

Bomb Laden

PERSONALITY:
Lively,
feisty

BALANCE:
Taut,
rigid

BODY:
Thin,
loose

BOUQUET:
Fruity,
tangy

LENGTH:
Reasonable,
satisfying

BURN RATING

💀💀💀

The Story

Bomb Laden comes complete with a hand-crafted turban and is perfect for reliving the events that led to Osama Bin Laden having his beardy, terrorist face blown off. Simply place the bottle inside a large box. This is Bin Laden's hideout. Place it next-door to a Pakistani military base. If there isn't one near you, a dry, dusty field will do. Now get yourself a gun. Run down to your local airfield, charter two helicopters, and instruct the pilots to fly to the hideout. Attach a webcam to your helmet so you can beam live pictures back to your mates. As you approach the hideout instruct one of the pilots to crash his helicopter (not the one you're in, the other one). Speed is now of the essence. The crash will have alerted others who may be rushing to assist. Don't shoot them. This is a re-enactment and they're probably nothing to do with Bin Laden. However, if any of them are wearing al-Qaeda T-shirts it's your shout.

Search the hideout thoroughly until you locate Bin Laden. Aim your gun at the handy crosshairs on the label and blow his face off. Now quickly pick up all the fragments and put into a cloth bag. Set fire to the crashed helicopter (check the pilot's not still in it) and get the hell out of there. Instruct the pilot to fly out to sea. On the way there prepare the fragments in the cloth bag to conform with Islamic precepts and practice. Chuck the cloth bag into the ocean and make your way home.
Mission accomplished.

Flavor notes:

A blend of fiery Habanero peppers, carrot, onion, and garlic with a tart vinegar and zesty lime finish. Decent heat that won't terrorize you too much.

PERSONALITY:
Lively, feisty

BALANCE:
Taut, rigid

BODY:
Thin, loose

BOUQUET:
Fruity, tangy

LENGTH:
Reasonable, satisfying

BURN RATING

☠☠☠

The Story

This sauce comes complete with a noose and is perfect for reliving the events that led to the snapping of Saddam Hussein's tyrannical neck. Firstly remove the noose from the bottle (keep it safe, you'll need it later). Saddam and you are pals for now. Use a big box to make a luxurious palace and place bottle inside. Visit Saddam in his palace and help him develop chemical weapons and approve billions in loan guarantees. This goes on for years, so fast forward to the bit where you decide that Saddam is actually a right bastard who's been stockpiling invisible weapons of mass destruction (not the ones you helped him develop). Remove Saddam from his palace and crush it.

Place Saddam on a brick to create a statue. Attach a rope to the back of your car and tie the other end around the statue. Drive forward slowly until the statue topples from the brick. Take your shoe off and hit the statue repeatedly (not too hard, it's a bottle remember). Now get someone to bury Saddam while you hide your eyes. Launch Operation Red Dawn and conduct a thorough search of your backyard until you locate Saddam hiding in his spider-hole. Make a prison cell using a small box and put Saddam inside whilst he awaits trial. Construct a set of gallows just in case you find him guilty. Find Saddam guilty. Reattach the noose that you removed earlier and fix it to the gallows. Use your phone to film yourself taking the piss prior to the hanging. Release the trapdoor in your gallows (if you haven't made a trapdoor, just nudge Saddam off the edge of a table). Post video on YouTube. Continue your search for WMDs.

Flavor notes:

Not quite a weapon of mass destruction but there is some decent heat from fiery Habanero peppers accompanied by a combination of carrot, garlic, onion, and lime.

Satan's Blood

The Story

Should you find yourself having a limb ripped off in a combine harvester accident or a major artery severed by a large shard of glass after being punched through a bar window by a drunken, steroid-fueled Neanderthal, then the chances are you're going to need a life-saving blood transfusion. For the chili addict, this can lead to major complications. Simply pumping normal blood that contains no capsaicin into a chilihead often proves such a shock to the system that it causes convulsions or, even worse, turns you into a dribbling wreck.

Trials are now being conducted using Satan's Blood for all transfusions carried out on chiliheads and the devil is regularly seen at his local blood donation center enjoying a cup of tea after donating his fiery claret. This has enraged religious leaders and caused at least 15 Jehovah's Witnesses to explode. Early results, however, seem to indicate that the blood of the devil, which consists of pure capsaicin, has proved highly effective in the treatment of chiliheads. Apart from in a couple of cases where they didn't get the dilution right and it dissolved the recipients' internal organs. And a few people have sprouted horns and cloven hooves. And one who terrorized a coach full of nuns whilst playing Ozzy Osbourne backward on his iPod.

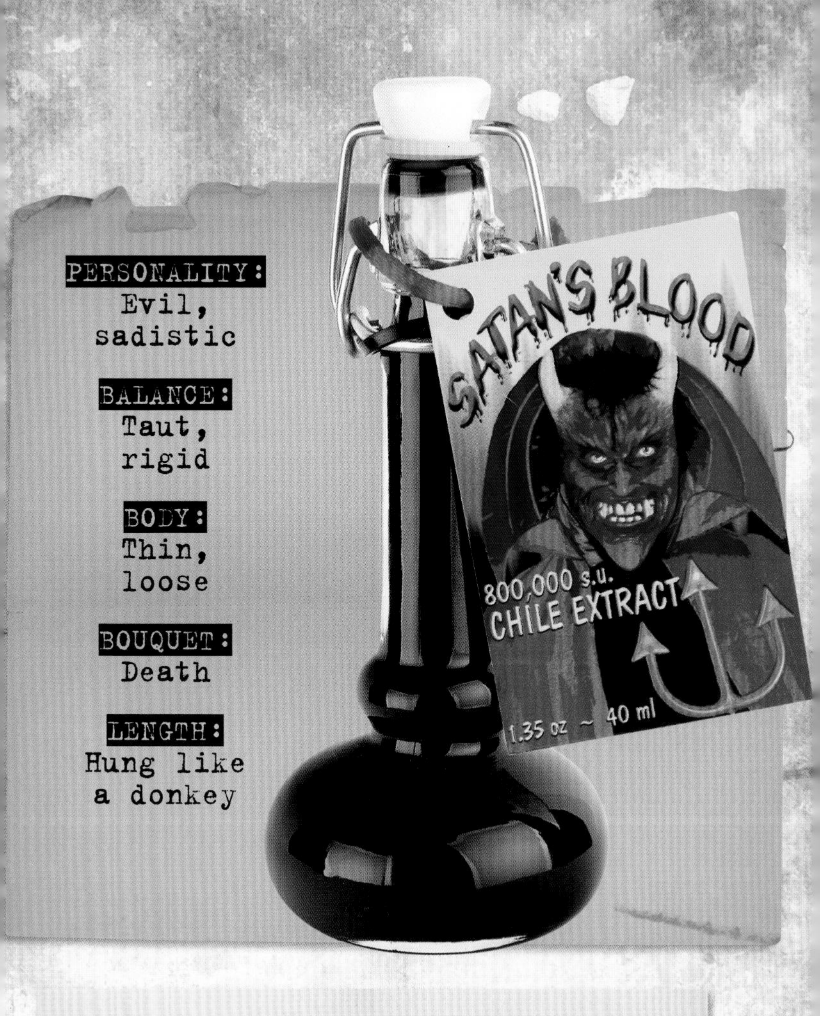

Flavor notes:

800,000 Scovilles of pure capsaicin extract suspended in red wine vinegar. Like licking the bowels of hell. Cooking additive only.

Crazy Jerry's Brain Damage

PERSONALITY:
Crazy,
bonkers

BALANCE:
Poised,
graceful

BODY:
Thin,
loose

BOUQUET:
Fruity,
sweet,
citrusy

LENGTH:
Well endowed,
good girth

BURN RATING

The Story

Subject: hot sauce tng
From: gangstamuthafcka@gangstamuthafcka.org
To: Dr. Burnorium

Yo Doc, LuvN da hot sauce tng U got goin on. My boy reckons he's a muthafckn gangsta & cn handL NEthing. cn U teL me a hot sauce dat wiL blo Hs nuts off cuz I wnt 2 c him squeal lIk I jst bust a cap n Hs (_!_).
Gangsta Muthafcka

Dear Gangsta, I'm sorry, but I haven't got a clue what you're saying. Are you human? If so, I think you may have sustained a serious head injury. Please go onto my website and buy a bottle of Crazy Jerry's Brain Damage. Get someone with a basic grasp of the English language and the ability to write proper words to do the address and stuff. When your sauce arrives, you'll notice that it has a bright pink plastic brain on top of the bottle. We'll use this for diagnostic purposes. First we need to expose your brain. Simply cut through the top of your skull with an angle-grinder and remove it. Now, using a mirror, check out the size and color of your brain. Don't tip your head too far forward or the contents might spill out. A healthy brain should be the size of an elephant's testicle and fluorescent green in color. Push your finger into it several times. It should be soft and squidgy. If your brain is no bigger than a human testicle, bright pink in color, and hard and plasticky to the touch like the one on the bottle, then you've definitely got brain damage and that is the reason you speak like a retard.

Flavor notes:

A mind-blowing concoction of scorching Habanero pepper combined within a fruity background of mandarin orange, mango, and honey, and finished with just a hint of garlic, Chipotle, and spices.

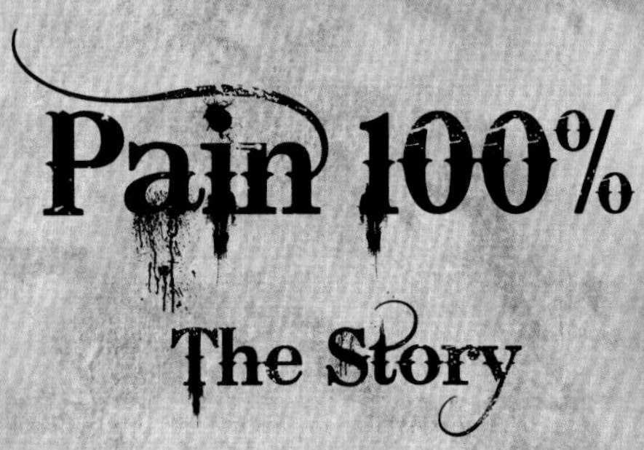

Pain 100%

The Story

Check out my handy Pain Percentage Comparison Chart.

20%—PERIOD PAIN: We all get a bit of a stomach ache at times. Just because there's blood involved doesn't mean it's any more painful. If you get a sudden nose bleed (not one caused by being punched in the face) does it actually hurt? No. And don't be so bloody cranky either.

40%—BACKDOOR EXCURSION: During intercourse the backdoor may be entered. No need for the dramatics. The average penis is no larger than a really big shit and you manage to squeeze them out without yelping and thrashing around like you've got a baseball bat rammed up your back passage.

60%—CHILDBIRTH: It might sting a bit, but it's only like having a big frontal dump. A lady's vagina is designed to stretch like a snake's jaw swallowing a wildebeest, so there's no need for all the puffing and panting and screaming.

70%—FAT MAN'S RUB (FMR): This painful chafing is caused by the rubbing together of sweaty, lard-filled thighs. FMR can cause such soreness in the region of the groin that sufferers have to adopt a bow-legged gait like they've got a cucumber stuck up their ass.

80%—STUBBED TOE: Little toe connects forcefully with immovable object. Time freezes. Air sucked from lungs. Heart bursts through chest Lights flash before eyes. A micro-second delay as brain acknowledges stubbing. Then there's the pain. The pain that's totally unique to a little toe. And screaming through gritted teeth you demand to know who left that fucking wardrobe there.

90%—FORESKIN IN ZIP: The moment that the end of your fleshy foreskin is bitten and secured between the teeth of a trouser zip can often lead to blind panic, nausea, and fainting. Your brain struggles to compute the enormity of the situation. You may start blubbering and whimpering like a small child. And then the horrific, stomach-churning realization that there's only one solution ...

100%—REMOVAL OF FORESKIN FROM ZIP

PERSONALITY:
Dangerous, murderous

BALANCE:
Rigid, poised

BODY:
Medium, trim

BOUQUET:
Tangy, fruity

LENGTH:
Eye watering

BURN RATING

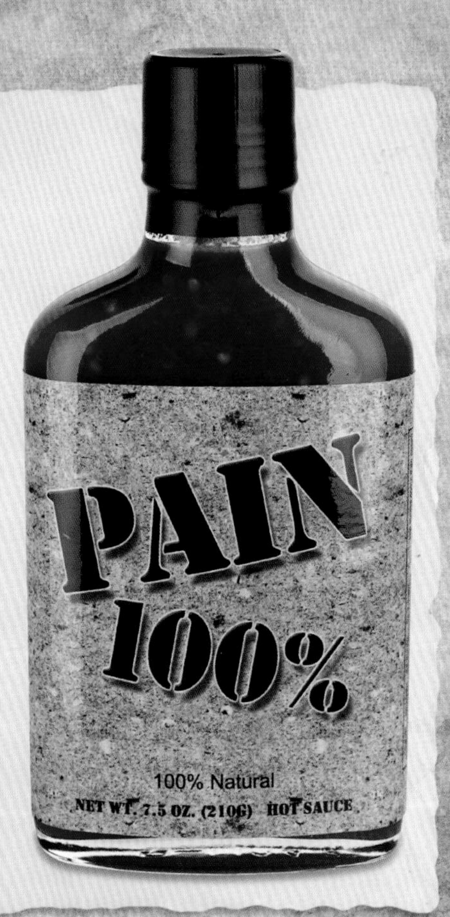

Flavor notes:

A rich tomato base that is absolutely packed with fiery Habanero peppers. The level of pain is increased with the addition of capsaicin extract. Not quite as painful as getting your foreskin caught in your zip but not far off.

Naga Soreass

The Story

In 1977 the legendary T. Rex died out following an incident involving a moving car and a stationary tree. Many experts believed this spelled extinction for the dinosaurs. For years just a handful clung to survival in the back yard of a struggling film director called Steven Spielberg. Back then Spielberg was penniless and his dream of opening a dinosaur theme park that could earn millions by charging 20.00 for a hot dog and a drink was about as likely as George Bush winning a pretzel-eating competition. This all changed when Spielberg met a portly English turkey farmer whose holy grail was to breed turkeys with a massive meat yield. He paid Spielberg enough cash to open his theme park in return for a big bucketful of dinosaur sperm with which he inseminated his turkeys. The resulting Turkeysaurus weighed in at nearly four tons with each breast the size of a **BMW 5 Series***.

In the past,the farmer's staff slaughtered turkeys by throwing them up in the air and playing baseball with them. Obviously the Turkeysaurus was way too big for that and would probably break their bats, so kissing and stroking to death in a loving manner became the preferred method of despatch. Once dead, the Turkeysaurus is pumped full of water to increase its weight to eight tons before being placed into a machine that hoovers all the meat, genitalia, toe nails, and eyelids from the carcass. The resulting goo is then lovingly mixed with lots of special, magic powders before being reformed into a whole range of cheap, delicious, nutritious Turkeysaurus products designed to satisfy the needs of the unemployed. Beautiful.

*Contains product placement. Manufacturer can send freebie c/o Dog 'n' Bone Books.

PERSONALITY:
Wild,
dangerous

BALANCE:
Poised,
elegant

BODY:
Thin,
loose

BOUQUET:
Fruity,
tangy,
spicy

LENGTH:
Well endowed,
good girth

BURN RATING

Flavor notes:

A wonderful blend of Red Savina Habanero and Naga Jolokia peppers rampaging through a well-spiced background of onion, tomatoes, garlic, and lemon.

Marie Sharp's Beware Comatose Heat Level

PERSONALITY:
Serious, forceful

BALANCE:
Poised, elegant

BODY:
Medium, trim

BOUQUET:
Tangy, fruity

LENGTH:
Well endowed, good girth

BURN RATING

💀💀💀💀

The Story

Just because you're paranoid doesn't mean they don't actually hate you. This sauce is the perfect way to find out. Simply dose yourself up and you'll lapse into a temporary 24-hour coma. To your family and hospital staff you'll resemble a brain-dead cabbage but, unbeknown to them, you'll still be fully aware of everything going on around you. Let the fun begin.

First at your bedside is your wife. She's willing you to just twitch a finger if you can hear her. Nothing. Your brother comes rushing in. Your distraught wife informs him that you're comatose and can't hear a thing. Your brother comforts her by sticking his tongue down her throat. The bastard! Before he's had a chance to go any further, your dad pokes his head round the door and tells your brother to ring him at the bar if you snuff it. Charming! Your mother arrives along with a nurse who proceeds to give you a bed bath. Your penis seems to amuse your mother. She tells your wife it's not really grown since you were a baby and she's not surprised she's screwing your brother if that's all you've got to offer. The bitch! The nurse says it looks like a maggot and flicks it. That's very unprofessional and needs reporting! Visiting time is over. Your family decide to join your dad for a few beers and leave. The nurse whispers in your ear. Apparently she is possessed by the spirit of serial killer Harold Shipman (aka Dr. Death) and needs to continue his work. Everything goes black as she pushes the pillow over your face. You try to twitch your finger. Nothing.

Flavor notes:

Trademark Marie Sharp's flavor of wonderful fruity Habanero within a background of carrot, onion, garlic, and lime. A dash of capsaicin extract cranks up the heat level but any harshness is well disguised with the addition of tomato and Cajun and Creole spices.

Thai Monkey

The Story

Just like their human counterparts, an increasing number of Thai monkeys are now involved in the sex trade. Prostitution is rife with jive-talking chimp pimps selling the sexual services of pretty young Thai monkeys to socially inadequate primates who visit Thailand from the West every year because they haven't got a hope in hell of ever getting laid in their own country. Unfortunately, Thai monkeys don't stay young and pretty forever and, at the first sign of wrinkles, their chimp pimps cast them aside like a used tissue in favor of newer, younger models. A few manage to scrape a living in seedy bars where they entertain drunken Western monkeys by firing ping-pong balls out of their snatch, but for many of the other specimens the only pole that they find themselves sliding down is the one that leads to a life of poverty. For this reason I'm proud to announce the launch of my charitable organization Monkey Relief. Together we can make a difference. Can you spare just 20.00 a month for Monkey Relief[1]? Every cent will go to those in need[2]. Not only will Monkey Relief give you a warm glow of satisfaction but just look at what you'll receive in return for your monthly donation:

FREE Personalized monkey adoption certificate[3]
FREE Monkey soft toy[4]
FREE Photograph of your chosen monkey with big sad eyes[5]
FREE Quarterly newsletter including medical updates[6]
FREE Ping-pong ball[7]

[1]Minimum contract term 120 months. Donations will be taken by Direct Debit. Failed payments may result in the death of your monkey.
[2]After the deduction of administration charges at least one cent from every dollar will be used for charitable purposes.
[3]Framed versions available for 49.95 + P&P.
[4]Not suitable for children. May be flammable and contain sharp bits. May have a limb missing. Stuffing may contain fiberglass or small insects.
[5]"Other" photographs 49.95 + P&P.
[6]We reserve the right to remove this if we can't be bothered to write one.
[7]May have been fired from a snatch.

PERSONALITY:
Friendly, cheeky

BALANCE:
Poised, elegant

BODY:
Medium, trim

BOUQUET:
Fruity, tangy, sweet

LENGTH:
Average, satisfying

BURN RATING

Flavor notes:

A cracking concoction that'll have you swinging through the trees like a very happy monkey. A rich base of teriyaki and soy with pineapple sweetness and a moderate kick of heat from Thai peppers and wasabi, finished with a subtly spiced background of peanut butter and garlic.

Widow No Survivors

PERSONALITY:
Deceitful, vicious

BALANCE:
Stable, rigid

BODY:
Medium, trim

BOUQUET:
Spicy, treacherous

LENGTH:
Hung like a donkey

BURN RATING

☠☠☠☠☠☠

The Story

Incy Wincy spider, climbed up the water spout,
Desperate for a cooling drink, to put the fire out,
His mouth it was aburning, tears in his eyes,
And all because the silly fool, put Widow on his flies.

The water spout was bone dry, it hadn't rained in days,
So Incy Wincy climbed back down, his mouth was still ablaze,
As he reached the drain below, a beauty lay within,
The sexiest thing he'd ever seen, a vision of spider sin.

Incy Wincy stood transfixed, lost in a lustful trance,
His heart it was a flutter, a lump within his pants,
The temptress reclined upon her web, legs open like a whore,
The cheeky minx was up for it, he couldn't fail to score.

Incy Wincy pumped away, his face turned crimson red,
But at the point he shot his load, her fangs were in his head,
Now Incy Wincy was being pumped, full of poisonous muck,
Black Widow whores don't come cheap, when you're dying for a fuck.

Black Widow spider, climbed up the water spout,
Desperate for a cooling drink, to put the fire out,
Her mouth it was a burning, tears in her eyes,
That's the last time she'd eat a punter, who'd put Widow on his flies.

Flavor notes:

A sturdy web of destruction with a tad of oriental influence courtesy of soy sauce and garlic which are ultimately devoured by the incredible heat of Habanero and capsaicin extract. Cooking additive only.

Ass in the Tub Armageddon

PERSONALITY:
Deadly,
apocalyptic

BALANCE:
Taut,
rigid

BODY:
Medium,
trim

BOUQUET:
Tangy,
damnation

LENGTH:
Hung like
a donkey

BURN RATING

☠☠☠☠☠☠

The Story

According to the Mayan calendar the world is going to end any day now and the only thing left will be cockroaches. Hold on. It might be nuclear war that cockroaches can survive. Not to worry, same thing. The main point is that Armageddon is upon us. Although, strictly speaking, Armageddon is more of a punch-up in a car park between God and his lot and Satan and his lot. Winner takes all. Anyway, the main thing is, come the day of reckoning, in whatever apocalyptic guise it manifests itself, the only thing left scuttling around this rock we call home will be cockroaches. And politicians. Same thing really.

The cockroaches will survive because they've got some kind of inbuilt indestructibility gene and politicians will survive because they've got a self-serving bastard gene. At the first sign of the shit hitting the fan they'll trample peasants underfoot to jump aboard their beloved gravy-train with a one-way ticket to Salvation Station situated in a lead-lined bunker three miles underground. The problem here is that once the dust has settled the politicians will once again emerge to take control. This is why we need to act now. Scientists need to take a break from growing ears on the backs of mice and start introducing a piranha gene into cockroaches. At least then, when the politicians do slither out of their bunker, sniffing the air for traces of oil, they'll get their smarmy faces chewed off.

Flavor notes:

Enough firepower to turn your bath into a hot-tub cum Jacuzzi. A combination of Habanero, Scotch Bonnet, and African oleoresin that will make it seem as if the world is ending directly through your ass. Cooking additive only.

Ass Reaper

The Story

True story. A lady walks into my store holding a dog lead attached to a spiked leather collar around the neck of a young man. Now, I've had some odd customers over the years, but this was definitely the first human dog. I wasn't sure if this contravened the "no dogs allowed" rule, but I figured I could turn a blind eye as long as he didn't crap on the floor. The lady picked up a bottle of Ass Reaper and enquired if the sauce would make someone suffer. I assured her that it would and advised her to go steady with it. The dog laughed. At this point the lady told me that the sauce was for a client and asked to use my laptop. Before I could even reply she'd all but barged me out of the way and was logging on to her website.

I suddenly became acutely aware that I was standing viewing hardcore pornography with a real-life dominatrix. She quickly clicked through various pictures of an S&M nature, pausing briefly at one of a person dressed head-to-toe in leather and wearing a gimp mask. This, she informed me, was her mother. Christmas must be a riot at their place. The picture she'd been looking for was now on display. Bending over a bench was a handcuffed, blindfolded bloke displaying his ass, the cheeks of which were so red and marked that it looked like he'd sat on a BBQ. I resisted the urge to ask if he was her dad. She told me in a sinister tone that he was the aforementioned client who the sauce was for. The significance of Ass Reaper dawned on me, as did the fact that it probably wasn't going to end up in his dinner.

BURN RATING

PERSONALITY:
Sadistic, domineering

BALANCE:
Taut, rigid

BODY:
Medium, trim

BOUQUET:
Tangy, damnation

LENGTH:
Hung like a donkey

Flavor notes:

A punishing and torturous blend of Habanero, Scotch Bonnet, and African oleoresin. Do not, under any circumstances, insert into any orifice other than a facial one. And, even then, only in very small amounts. Cooking additive only.

Sphincter Shrinker

PERSONALITY:
Crazy, dangerous

BALANCE:
Poised, taut

BODY:
Medium, trim

BOUQUET:
Fruity, curry

LENGTH:
Well endowed good girth

BURN RATING

☠☠☠☠☠

The Story

For chiliheads, there are few things as annoying as a baggy sphincter. If this small but powerful muscle malfunctions it can cause a whole host of problems, including "persistent expulsion"—a constant hissing that sounds like a gas leak and often leads to the evacuation of buildings. Very embarrassing for the sufferer. The usual method of treating a baggy sphincter was with a wine-bottle cork, but this merely masked the issue rather than solved it. What was needed was something that actually tightened the sphincter back into good working order.

The solution was found by Professor Payne Indeass when a lady with whom he was having sex suddenly had a seizure and her muscles contracted to such an extent that it took a pound of butter and a crowbar to free himself. After much research the professor isolated the spasm chemical and discovered it occurred naturally in raisins; hence their shriveled appearance. Early versions of the professor's raisin treatment were applied internally, but not only did this make your finger stink, it also left your house looking as though it had a rodent infestation if they weren't inserted to a sufficient depth. It was then that the professor hit on the idea of adding the raisin treatment to a product that would appeal to the biggest sufferers, namely chiliheads. Professor Payne Indeass' Sphincter Shrinker hot sauce, complete with raisins, was born.

Flavor notes:

Quite an unusual, apple-based sauce with a cracking blend of Indian-style curry spices and raisins, all topped off with pure capsaicin extract to really fire the heat level up.

Blair's Sudden Death

The Story

Dear Dr. Burnorium,
Despite the fact that my wife knows I have a phobia of animals sh bought the kids a pet. I'm a nervous wreck and now have problems sustaining an erection. Can you suggest anything to help? **Trevor**

Dear Trevor,
Well, you could despatch it with a shovel. But, then again, you'd still have the pet problem. I jest. You need to make it look like an accident. I think your best bet is a bottle of Blair's Sudden Death. A good lug of this stuff in your pet's food should do the trick, and it'll look like natural causes. You don't say what animal it is but I reckon one teaspoon of Sudden Death would equat to one good hard whack with a shovel. So, one should suffice for something small like a hamster. A cat will probably need two. Thre to be on the safe side. We'll skip dogs, because they're man's bes friend and no sane person would ever consider harming one. Unless it's one of those yappy, scrawny things that celebrities carry around like a designer handbag, in which case give it three. And one for luck. Anything bigger like a goat and you'll have to play it by ear. Naturally your kids will get a bit tearful when they find out their beloved pet has "passed away peacefully" in the night, but they should cheer up a bit when you let them use the coffin box that your Sudden Death came in to bury it. A hamster will fit in fine, but you might have to chop a cat into small pieces. Goat you've got no chance. As for your erection problem, Sudden Death can help there, too. It contains ginseng, a powerful aphrodisiac. DO NOT apply directly to your penis. Just add a drop to your food (not too much, we don't want you going the same way a your pet) and you'll be hard as nails in no time.

PERSONALITY:
Evil,
murderous

BALANCE:
Rigid,
poised

BODY:
Medium,
trim

BOUQUET:
Tangy,
death

LENGTH:
Hung like
a donkey

BURN RATING

Flavor notes:

A crazy concoction of Habanero and Cayenne peppers set within a background of honey, garlic, lime, and a tad of ginseng. Whilst the ginseng may put a bit of lead in your pencil the intense heat of the capsaicin extract will definitely put a fire in your belly. Cooking additive only.

Mad Dog 357

PERSONALITY:
Insane, dangerous

BALANCE:
Twisted, unstable

BODY:
Medium, trim

BOUQUET:
Tangy, vengeful

LENGTH:
Impressive weapon with a hell of a range

BURN RATING

☠☠☠☠☠☠

The Story

In the second extract from Mad Dog's autobiography, **Mad Dog: Cross Me and I'll Take Your Face Off***, he tells how he was once again shafted by the entertainment industry.

"The walls of the Hanna Barbera Studios were lined with photos of some of the most famous dogs in TV history: Huckleberry Hound, Mutley, Droopy. And now I'd be joining them. I was Scooby-Doo, the star of a new show that had hit written all over it. Suddenly I was accosted by a security guard asking where I was going. "I'm with them," I replied, pointing to my co-stars Fred, Daphne, Velma, and Shaggy who were stood with a big, dumb-looking dog. The guard asked if they knew me. They all shook their heads. "I'm Scooby-Doo," I protested. "I'm Rooby-Roo," said the dog. "I think he needs to leave the premises," said Velma. I couldn't believe it. It was like The Beatles all over again. Only now I'd been replaced by a dog with a speech impediment. I did what anyone would have done in the circumstances. I pulled out my weapon. Daphne fainted, Velma puked. With the girls distracted I now pulled out my Magnum 357 gun. Fred soiled his flares and Rooby-fucking-Roo ran off like a pussy. Shaggy didn't move, he seemed a bit out of it. Anyway, the next thing I knew I was in hospital with a doctor telling me I had major problems. Damn right I had. I'd lost the gig. He suggested I see a psychiatrist but I didn't need someone who could see into the future to tell me that, once again, I'd been shafted."

Flavor notes:

A fearsome weapon loaded with the ballistic madness of Habanero and Cayenne peppers topped with enough capsaicin extract to blow your face off. Please take care when handling your weapon. Cooking additive only.

*14.95—available from all good bookshops

Ass Blaster
The Story

June 25th 2009 is certainly one of those dates that stands out in history, for it was on this day that the plastic-faced Peter Pan of pop Michael Jackson died alone in his bed. A tsunami of shock reverberated around the world. The whole planet shook its head in disbelief. But it was true. He was alone in his bed. This, however, wasn't the only celebrity death on June 25th 2009. As Michael Jackson's doctor was frantically trying to resurrect the King of Pop, the beautiful (Charlie's) Angel that was Farrah Fawcett sadly also passed away.

All of this obviously put a bit of a dampener on George Michael's birthday, which was also on June 25th 2009 (as well as all the other years from 1963 onward). Not only had he lost a friend and fellow pop-star, but he'd also lost the woman who inspired his hairstyle when he was in Wham. Obviously a traumatic time for George and that's probably why I never got so much as a 'thank you' for the hot sauce that I sent him for his birthday. I can't think of any other reason. I thought if anyone would appreciate an Ass Blaster in an outside toilet then it would be George. I even put a little figure of a cop inside the box.

PERSONALITY:
Angry, cantankerous

BALANCE:
Rigid, poised

BODY:
Slim, loose

BOUQUET:
Tangy, fruity

LENGTH:
Hung like a donkey

Flavor notes:

Fruity Habanero peppers and tart vinegar combined with carrot, garlic, and spices. A generous dash of capsaicin extract will have you kicking the bathroom door off its hinges before enduring a serious ass-blasting experience.

Holy Shit!

PERSONALITY:
Crucifying, blasphemous

BALANCE:
Rigid, upright

BODY:
Medium, trim

BOUQUET:
Tangy, not shitty

LENGTH:
Hung like a donkey

BURN RATING

The Story

It seems that the image of Christ is now appearing with alarming regularity on all manner of everyday objects. Scarcely a day goes by without someone noticing the face of Jesus burnt into a slice of toast or grinning back at them from a piece of liver or a dog's backside. One such occurrence of this phenomenon has become known as Peter's Pan. In this case, however, it wasn't charred food remnants in a frying pan that produced a holy image, but rather a mark on a toilet pan belonging to a hot sauce fan called Peter. This was undoubtedly caused by the forceful impact of the "turtles head," a short piece of solid waste that acts as a floodgate to the more liquid stuff.

Although it gives chiliheads a fighting chance of getting to the toilet before they actually shit themselves, the "turtles head" is often jettisoned at incredibly high speeds and this leads to stubborn staining when it ricochets off the toilet pan. As Peter stood there contemplating how many well-directed jets of piss it was going to take to shift the skid-mark he noticed a face staring back at him. On closer inspection it became apparent that this wasn't just any old face, but the most holy of all faces. The likeness was unmistakeable. There before Peter in all his majestic, Godly, saintliness was Bono, complete with brown wrap-around shades. Holy shit indeed.

Flavor notes:

A background of tomato, onion, and garlic cranked to the extreme with the addition of pure capsaicin extract. This stuff will have you creating your own iconic images before you know it.

Crazy Jerry's Mustard Gas

PERSONALITY:
Explosive, blistering

BALANCE:
Rigid, taut

BODY:
Medium, trim

BOUQUET:
Mustardy, tangy

LENGTH:
Well endowed, good girth

BURN RATING

The Story

Many of the world's greatest inventions have come about by accident. One of the most famous examples is a product invented by some bloke who had trouble removing the dried shit from the fur around his dog's arse. When examined under a microscope he noticed that the clag-nuts had tiny little "hooks" that attached the shit so securely to the "loops" in his dog's fur that they were virtually impossible to remove. This eureka moment gave birth to Velcro. Another famous example was for a form of packaging that transformed the shipping of delicate objects. Bizarrely, this idea originated from mustard.

In ancient times mustard seed was given as a love token during courtship. I'm not sure if the subliminal context was that you wanted to plant your seed into something moist and warm, but it does seem a more romantic way of getting into someone's pants than the modern day equivalent of cider and cheap wine. Anyway, during the First World War a peace-loving, hippy German scientist secretly filled bombs with mustard gas in the belief that it would spread love and bring an end to the conflict. Unfortunately for him it all went a bit tits-up, and the mustard gas caused horrendous injuries with victims suffering burns that produced huge blisters all over their bodies. This led to a eureka moment from one particularly astute nurse who'd recently received a broken teapot in the post, and thus Bubble Wrap was born.

Flavor notes:

A highly effective weapon packed with mustard seed, garlic, and onion accompanied by a seriously explosive charge of pure capsaicin extract.

Iguana En Fuego

PERSONALITY:
Fiery,
blazing

BALANCE:
Poise,
elegant

BODY:
Full,
muscular

BOUQUET:
Fruity,
tangy

LENGTH:
Fire fighter's
hosepipe

BURN RATING

☠☠☠☠☠

The Story

If you're English, learning a foreign language is pointless. All but the most lazy of foreigners speak English, so why bother mastering a mind-boggling array of alien words? If you need to talk to someone who hasn't had the courtesy to learn English, then speaking louder and slower whilst using hand gestures will do the trick. The only exception to this rule is when, by learning a foreign phrase, you could save a child's life. For this reason, it is vital that all responsible parents buy a bottle of Iguana En Fuego.

Although the word Iguana looks foreign, it's not; it's English for "lizard with a flicky tongue." En Fuego on the other hand is Spanish. And it's a phrase you need to teach your kids if you want them to escape a house fire. Especially when said fire occurs whilst they're under the care of a Hispanic babysitter who's unable to speak English.

Alerted by a burning smell, your children start frantically screaming "Fire!" There is no response from the babysitter downstairs, to whom the words are just foreign noise. "Fire!" they scream again. Nothing. The eldest kid suddenly remembers the foreign phrase on the bottle of Iguana and the fact that the babysitter is Spanish. Your responsible parenting has paid off. "En Fuego! En Fuego!" they scream. The babysitter's Spanish ears now detect perfectly the words "On Fire! On Fire!", because that is exactly what En Fuego means. She rescues your children from danger, which makes her a bit of a hero, but the true hero is your lifesaving bottle of Iguana En Fuego.

Flavor notes:

A seriously scorching combination of Habanero peppers and pure capsaicin extract within a base of carrot, onion, and garlic enhanced with fruity pineapple, papaya, passion fruit, and lime.

Blair's Pure Death

The Story

Unfortunately, when most people with an interest in world politics see the word BLAIR their brain immediately pukes up sickly images of an ex-prime minister whose smug, lying bastard face could easily out-grin a Cheshire cat enjoying the best blowjob ever. I'd therefore like to make it perfectly clear that this sauce has got nothing whatsoever to do with Tony Blair. It definitely isn't produced by the guy who surrounded himself with spinning sycophants who had their tongues so far up his ass that they could lick the back of his eyeballs clean. It definitely isn't produced by the guy who ordered British troops into battle more times than any prime minster in history. It's not made by the guy whose cozy relationship with the world's most powerful media tycoon led to him becoming Godfather to one of Rupert Murdoch's daughters. It definitely isn't produced by the guy who cashes in on the position he once held to earn £100,000 a pop for public speaking gigs. It definitely isn't made by the guy whose company declared an income of £12 million in 2011 but only paid £315,000 in corporation tax, having written off nearly £11 million as "administrative expenses." No. It definitely isn't made by that guy. It is in fact made by Blair Lazar, one of the finest hot sauce makers in the USA. So, I hope that this clears things up for the morons who come into my shop and ask if this sauce is made by Tony Blair. Just as a side note, this actually got me wondering if the potential for brand confusion worked the other way around. If the UK electronics company Bush sold their stuff in the USA, would Yank brains regurgitate images of the pretzel-choking chimp who used to run the country? Or, like me, would they think of hairy vaginas?

PERSONALITY:
Lively,
feisty

BODY:
Full,
muscular

BALANCE:
Graceful,
elegant

BOUQUET:
Fruity,
tangy

LENGTH:
Average,
satisfying

BURN RATING

Flavor notes:

Pure, simple, and absolutely delicious. Beautiful fiery Habanero fruitiness with just a tad of Naga Jolokia pepper, a touch of salt, and a splash of vinegar. That's it. Four ingredients blended to perfection. Sometimes less is more and this is a prime example.

Psycho Juice 70% Habanero

PERSONALITY:
Lively, feisty

BODY:
Full, muscular

BALANCE:
Poised, elegant

LENGTH:
Average, satisfying

BOUQUET:
Fruity, tangy

BURN RATING

Flavor notes:

Incredible, fruity, full-bodied Habanero flavor with a background of naturally sweet carrot, a touch of onion and garlic, and a citrusy blast of lemon juice.

The Story

OK. Now I'm a multi-award-winning author, I figured that my legions of adoring fans might like to read the official autobiography of yours truly. I am therefore writing the warts-and-all account of my really interesting life, minus all the boring bits that nobody's interested in, like childhood and school and parents. Why do people feel the need to write about that? Just get to the interesting bits for fuck's sake. Anyway, I've pitched the idea to my current publisher and told them that because of the massive worldwide success of this book I'll be looking for a five-figure advance. Their offer of 127.95 is admittedly five-figures, but it's not exactly what I had in mind. Well, they've had their chance and, as much as I've enjoyed working with them, I'm afraid I'm going to have to open this up to other publishing companies who are undoubtedly tracking my writing career with fevered interest. For them I offer the brief synopsis below. Let the bidding war commence.

Synopsis
They swore I was Jack. The hangman's noose was to seal my fate. With the pack closing in I abandoned all that I held dea**r** and fled deep into the putrid underbelly of a d**e**bauched city. Here I met Sal**v**ia, an escaped freak-show dwarf, who told of his addiction to a ferociously fi**e**ry fruit that contained an incredible, pain-i**n**ducing capsaicin compound capable of causin**g** the release of opiate-bas**e**d endorphins from **w**ithin the human brain. To extract, crystallize, and **i**mbibe the endorphins of others, Sa**l**via insisted, would be to unlock the secret of our immorta**l**ity. But first we had to inflict the pain. A pact was duly made and together we em**b**arked upon our mission to incin**e**rate the living. My accusers had branded **m**e a psycho and now, in the name of all that I had lost, psycho they would get. From a d**i**sused crematorium, Salvia and I co**n**cocted an array of amazing fiery products capable of producing the pr**e**cious endorphins from within the brains of our victims. Eternal life would now be ours.

Fear

PERSONALITY:
Serious, scary

BALANCE:
Poised, elegant

BODY:
Medium, trim

BOUQUET:
Fruity, tangy

LENGTH:
Well endowed

BURN RATING

The Story

Nyctophobes fear the dark, they do not like the night
Phengophobes fear the day, they do not like the light
Ornithophobes fear all birds, maybe they'll get pecked
Phallophobes fear men's cocks, especially when erect
Agyrophobes hate crossing roads
Bufonophobes are scared of toads
Urophobes don't like piss
Luiphobes fear syphilis
Defecaloesiophobes fear shitting, the movement of the bowel
Alektorophobes fear chickens, they really think they're fowl
Coulrophobes fear circus clowns, to them they're just not funny
Chrometophobes fear what most desire: dirty, filthy money
Myrmecophobes can't cope with ants
Chorophobes are afraid to dance
Genuphobes are scared of knees
Rectophobes fear bum disease
Staurophobes fear the crucifix, it's a cross they have to bear
Peladophobes fear balding men with very little hair
Chronophobes fear clocks, they never know the time
Metrophobes fear poetry; the crafted, written rhyme
And with that in mind I'll finish now and, as I fade to black,
Somewhere a Metrophobe is reading this and having a panic attack.

Flavor notes:

Top notch Naga Jolokia pepper flavor within a carrot, onion, and garlic background enhanced with papaya, passion fruit, and lime juice.

the recipes

Psycho Con Carne

INGREDIENTS (Serves 6)

3 tbsp olive oil
3 lbs (1.4 kg) beef chuck, cut into ½ in. (1 cm) cubes
4 medium onions, finely chopped
4 fresh red chilies, finely chopped
8 garlic cloves, minced
1 lb (450g) ground (minced) beef
2 tbsp Ancho chili powder
2 tbsp New Mexico chili powder
2 tbsp ground cumin
1 tbsp ground coriander
2 tbsp Hungarian paprika
1 tbsp Mexican oregano
1 tbsp Mexican cocoa
2 tsp black pepper
2 tsp salt
2 x 14 oz (400 g) cans chopped tomatoes
2 tbsp Ghost Pepper-based hot sauce (I used Psycho Juice 70%)
3 tbsp smoked hot sauce (I used Psycho Juice Smoked Ghost Pepper)
1 pint (550 ml) beef stock
1 pint (550 ml) beer
2 tbsp red wine vinegar
2 x 15 oz (400 g) cans red kidney beans or black beans
1 tbsp masa harina (optional)
Chopped red onion, grated mature cheddar, and sour cream, to serve

Few dishes in the culinary world have provoked such fiery debate as chili (or chilli, or chile, or chilli con carne, or chili con carne). To bean or not to bean may be the question, but it's only one of many. The one thing upon which most chili aficionados will agree is that, contrary to popular belief, chili—whichever way you want to spell it—is not a Mexican dish and actually originates from Texas, USA. The key to creating a fantastic Bowl 'o Red lies in a long, slow cooking process and, of course, the ingredients. Cheaper, tougher cuts of beef work best, plenty of cumin is essential, and without some serious chili fire you may as well just cook a beef stew. Treat a chili with the love and respect it deserves and you'll be rewarded with a dish that epitomizes heart, soul, fire, and flavor.*

Method

1. Pour the olive oil into a large, heavy-based pan and get it nice and hot. Add the cubed beef chuck in small batches and brown. Remove with a slotted spoon and set aside.

2. Put your onions, chilies, and garlic into the pan and sweat until they are soft. Add the ground beef and brown.

3. Put the beef chuck back into pan with the ground beef, onions, garlic, and chili mixture. Lower the heat and add the chili powders, cumin, coriander, paprika, oregano, cocoa, black pepper, and salt, stirring well to coat the meat.

4. Add the chopped tomatoes and hot sauces. Stir well. Pour in the beef stock, beer, and vinegar. Crank up the heat and bring to the boil. Stir occasionally to stop the chili catching on the bottom of the pan. Once at the boil, turn the heat down as low as it will go. You want just a few bubbles breaking the surface. Leave the lid off. This will allow the moisture to escape and your chili to thicken naturally.

5. Cook on a low heat for 2½–3 hours until your beef is fall-apart tender. Stir regularly to stop the chili catching. Body is crucial. You want your chili to be the consistency of good-quality ketchup. Too thick, and you can loosen it by adding water. Too thin, and you can cook for longer or thicken with the masa harina mixed into water.

6. Texans look away now. Once the chili is at a consistency you're happy with, add the beans and stir into the chili. Serve topped with red onion, grated cheddar, and a blob of sour cream.

*Note: If you want to make a milder chili, then cut back on the fiery ingredients and hot sauce.

Simple Psycho Ribs

There are those who have dedicated their lives to cooking the perfect ribs. Such passion has to be respected and I for one think these culinary mavericks are a special breed. If you've never cooked ribs before, then this is a pretty simple recipe that will give you an insight into what can be achieved. Feel free to tinker with the rub ingredients and just cut back on the chili stuff if you don't want it so fiery.

INGREDIENTS (Serves 2-3)

3 lb (1.3 kg) pork baby back ribs
2 tbsp vegetable oil

For the rub:
2 tbsp Cayenne pepper
1 tbsp Chipotle chili powder
2 tbsp brown sugar
2 tbsp Superfine (caster) sugar
2 tbsp paprika
1 tbsp garlic powder
1 tbsp salt
½ tbsp black pepper
½ tbsp ginger
½ tbsp onion powder
½ tbsp rosemary powder

For the baste:
2 cups BBQ sauce (I used Fat Bastard Gourmet Billy B Damned)
1 tbsp smoked hot sauce (I used Psycho Juice Smoked Ghost Pepper)

Method

1. Remove the membrane from the ribs. Please do this, as it makes a big difference. Slide a butter knife under the membrane and lift. Tease the membrane loose with your fingers and pull it clean off.

2. Combine all the ingredients for the rub in a bowl.

3. Rub the ribs with vegetable oil. Sprinkle both sides of the ribs with the rub. Wrap the ribs in foil and put in the fridge for at least an hour or two, overnight if possible.

4. Preheat your oven to 275°F (135°C) and cook the ribs low and slow in their foil for about 4 hours.

5. Mix the hot sauce with the BBQ sauce.

6. Get a grill, or preferably a charcoal BBQ, good and hot. Remove the ribs from the foil and grill them for 5–10 minutes while brushing with the BBQ sauce until well colored and caramelized.

Psycho Fajitas

Fajitas not only taste fantastic, they're also a great social way of eating. If you cook them on a heavy griddle pan you can plonk it on the table and just let everyone dig in. If not, then just serve from dishes. The important bit is that everyone helps themselves and builds their fajitas exactly how they want them. If you can, make the guacamole in the recipe—it's so much better than the stuff you can buy.

INGREDIENTS (Serves 4)

4 x ½ lb (225 g) sirloin steaks
5 tbsp olive oil
1 tbsp paprika
1 tbsp ground cumin
1 tbsp smoked hot sauce (I used Psycho Juice Smoked Ghost Pepper)
Juice of half a lime
Salt and black pepper
2 red onions, quartered, layers pulled apart.
1 large red bell pepper, thinly sliced
8 tortillas

For the guacamole:
3 ripe avocados
1 large tomato
1 red onion, finely chopped
1 fresh red chili, finely chopped
Handful of fresh cilantro (coriander), chopped
Juice of a lime

Serve with sour cream, grated cheese, hot sauce (I used Psycho Juice 70% Red Savina), and lime juice.

Method

1. Put 3 tbsp olive oil in a large bowl and stir in the paprika, cumin, smoked hot sauce, and lime juice. Season with a good sprinkle of salt and black pepper.

2. Cut the steak into ½ in. (1cm) strips, add to the bowl of spice mix, and coat thoroughly with the spiced oil. Cover the bowl and whack it in the fridge for an hour.

3. Meanwhile, make your guacamole. Halve and stone the avocados (save the stone, it helps to stop the guacamole going brown). Scoop out the flesh with a spoon and put into a bowl.

4. Finely chop the tomato (you want it pretty much pulverized). Stick it in the bowl with the avocado. Add the red onion, chili, cilantro, and lime juice and season with salt and pepper. Mash everything together with a fork until you have a chunky texture. Put the reserved stone in the bowl, cover with plastic wrap, and whack it in the fridge until needed.

5. Put the remaining 2 tbsp olive oil in a large frying pan or a heavy griddle pan and get it nice and hot. Using tongs, add the strips of steak to the pan, plus the onions and bell peppers. Keep turning until cooked and nicely caramelized. Season with salt and pepper.

6. Heat the tortillas in a preheated oven, microwave, or dry frying pan.

7. Top each tortilla with meat, onions, and red peppers. Add a good dollop of guacamole and sour cream and finish off with a squirt of lime juice, a sprinkling of grated cheese, and a splash of hot sauce.

Psycho Huevos Rancheros with Chorizo

INGREDIENTS (Serves 4)

2 tbsp olive oil
1 red onion, diced
2 cloves garlic, minced
2 fresh green chilies, finely chopped
3½ oz (100 g) chorizo, diced
1-14 oz (400 g) can chopped tomatoes
1 tbsp Red Savina hot sauce (I used Psycho Juice 70%)
¼ cup (10 g) fresh cilantro (coriander), finely chopped
Salt and black pepper
1 lime, halved
1-14 oz (400 g) can refried beans
4 corn tortillas
4 eggs
1 fresh red chili, thinly sliced
1 scallion (spring onion), thinly sliced

I'm not a big breakfast person. Coffee and cigarettes normally do the trick. However, there are few things better than Huevos Rancheros to start your day and the chili is guaranteed to put a spring in your step. Of course, you don't just have to have this for breakfast—it's good at any time of the day.

Method

1. Heat the oil in a frying pan and fry the onion, garlic, and green chilies until soft. Add the chorizo and fry until nicely colored.

2. Put the tomatoes into the pan. Crank the heat up and add Psycho Juice 70% Red Savina hot sauce and about three quarters of the cilantro. Season with salt and black pepper to taste and blast a good squirt of the juice of half a lime into your tomato salsa. Reduce heat to a decent simmer and cook for a good 15–20 minutes until the mixture starts to thicken.

3. While your tomato salsa is cooking, heat your refried beans gently in a separate pan.

4. If you want to do your tortillas in the oven, get it pre-heated to about 425°F (220°C) and place them on a rack for about 10 minutes. Otherwise you can just zap them in the microwave or toast them directly in a hot dry pan. Your shout.

5. In a separate pan, fry your eggs in a splash of oil.

6. To serve, put a tortilla on a plate and spread on a quarter of the refried beans. Spoon your tomato salsa on top of the refried beans and top with a fried egg. Spoon more tomato salsa on top of the egg. Garnish with the remaining cilantro, slices of red chili, scallions, and the other half of the lime, cut into wedges.

Psycho Corned Beef Hash

There's only one thing better than good old-fashioned comfort food and that's good old-fashioned comfort food with a belt of chili heat. If you've never had corned beef hash topped with a fried egg before then give it a go—you'll be glad that you did. If you want less heat, just use less fiery stuff.

INGREDIENTS (Serves 4)

1¼ cups (250 g) new potatoes, cut into ¾ in. (2 cm) cubes
1 tbsp olive oil
1 onion, diced
1 garlic clove, minced
4 fresh red chilies, finely chopped
3½ tbsp butter
8 oz (225 g) corned beef, cut into ¾ in. (2 cm) cubes
2 tbsp hot sauce (I used Psycho Juice Smoked Ghost Pepper)
2 tbsp Worcestershire sauce
Salt and black pepper
2 tbsp parsley, finely chopped
4 eggs

Method

1. Boil your potatoes in a pan of salted water for about 8 minutes. Drain, cover, and set aside.

2. Whack the olive oil into a large pan and fry the onions, garlic, and chilies until softened and lightly browned.

3. Push the onion, garlic, and chili mix to one side in the pan. Add the butter and fry your drained potatoes until tender and golden.

4. While your potatoes are frying, mix the corned beef, hot sauce, and Worcestershire sauce together in a bowl. Season with salt and black pepper.

5. Add the corned beef mixture to your pan of potatoes, onions, garlic, and chilies. Mix well and fry until everything is well heated. Add the parsley and stir in.

6. Once heated, dish out and top each portion with a fried egg.

Psycho Meatloaf

As you'd expect, my version of meatloaf has got a good fiery kick to it. If you don't want it so spicy, just use less chili or Psycho Juice hot sauce. I make mine with a combination of ground beef and Cumberland sausage meat, but you can use all beef if you'd prefer. This is great hot or cold.

INGREDIENTS (Serves 4-6)

Olive oil
2 onions, finely chopped
1 carrot, finely chopped
1 celery stick, finely chopped
4 fresh red chilies, finely chopped
2 garlic cloves, minced
14 oz (400 g) ground (minced) beef
14 oz (400 g) sausage meat
¾ cup (100 g) breadcrumbs
2 tbsp Parmesan cheese
5 tbsp ketchup
2 tbsp hot sauce (I used Psycho Juice Mustard Ghost Pepper)
1 tbsp Worcestershire sauce
1 egg, beaten
Handful fresh parsley, finely chopped
2 tsp thyme
2 tsp Mexican oregano
Salt and black pepper
10 rashers bacon

Method

1. Pre-heat your oven to 400°F (200°C).

2. Whack a good lug of olive oil into a large pan and get it nice and hot. Add the onions, carrot, celery, chilies, and garlic. Sauté them until softened and transfer to large bowl.

3. Into the bowl add your beef, sausage meat, breadcrumbs, Parmesan cheese, 3 tbsp of the ketchup, Psycho Juice hot sauce, Worcestershire sauce, egg, parsley, thyme, and oregano. Season with a good sprinkle of salt and black pepper.

4. Mix thoroughly with your hands until all the ingredients are well combined.

5. Line a 10 x 5 in. (25 x 12.5 cm) loaf tin with the rashers of bacon and firmly pack with the meat mixture. Spread the rest of the ketchup over the top of the meat.

6. Bang it in the pre-heated oven and bake for about 1 hour until cooked completely through to the center of the meatloaf.

7. Remove from the oven and allow to stand for 10 minutes before slicing.

8. Great served hot with mashed potatoes and lovely when cold and sliced into crusty rolls with an extra splash of hot sauce.

Psycho Burger with Gentleman's Relish

Everyone loves a good burger. They tend to get a bad press at times but when you go to the effort of making your own they're a million miles away from the generic commercial offerings. Feel free to play around with the ingredients. There ain't no rules—add whatever you fancy. Obviously, mine come complete with a healthy dose of heat but if you want it milder, lower the chili ingredients.

INGREDIENTS (Serves 4-6)

For the burgers:

2 lb 2 oz (1 kg) ground (minced) beef
Handful of breadcrumbs
Handful of flat-leaf parsley, finely chopped
3 tbsp grated Parmesan
1 red onion, finely chopped
4 fresh red chili peppers, finely chopped
2 cloves garlic, minced
1 large egg
3 tbsp mustard-based hot sauce (I used Psycho Juice Mustard Ghost Pepper)
Salt and black pepper
Olive oil
6 burger buns
1 lettuce, washed*
3 tomatoes, sliced
1 red onion, sliced

For the Gentleman's Relish:

1 cup (220g) mayonnaise
2 tsp smoked hot sauce (I used Psycho Juice Smoked Ghost Pepper)
2 pickled gherkins, finely chopped

*Always shake your lettuce to get rid of excess moisture, right ladies?

Method

1. Put the ground beef, breadcrumbs, parsley, and Parmesan in a large bowl.

2. Add the red onion, chili, and garlic to the bowl. Crack in the egg and add the hot sauce. Add a good sprinkle of salt and black pepper to season.

3. Mix the ingredients thoroughly with your hands. Get it well scrunched up. The sauce is hot, so you might want to wear gloves. If you choose not to, then don't come whinging to me when you rub your eye or scratch your genitalia later.

4. Shape into 4–6 burgers, depending on how big you want them. They should be about 1 in. (2.5 cm) thick. Drizzle burgers with a bit of olive oil, cover, and bang them in the fridge for an hour to allow them to firm up.

5. Get a frying pan or griddle good and hot. Reduce the heat and cook your burgers about 5 minutes each side depending on how you like them done.

6. While the burgers are cooking, make the Gentleman's Relish by stirring the hot sauce and pickled gherkins into the mayonnaise.

7. Cut your burger buns in half and lightly toast them. Spread buns with Gentleman's Relish and add your burger, lettuce, tomato, and red onion. Feel free to top with more Gentleman's Relish and hot sauce.

Pulled Pork Psycho Sandwich

The secret to pulled pork is a really long and slow cook. The low cooking temperature and the fat in the pork shoulder keep the meat succulent. When it is literally fall-apart tender you know it's done. Please use a good-quality BBQ sauce—it makes a big difference. If you're a bit of a wimp when it comes to heat, just use less of the fiery stuff.

INGREDIENTS (Serves 4–6)

1 tbsp paprika
1 tbsp Mexican oregano
1 tbsp ground cumin
2 tbsp Cayenne pepper
1 tsp salt
1 tsp black pepper
3 tbsp olive oil
1½ lb (1 kg) pork shoulder, deboned
8 oz (250 ml) BBQ sauce (I used Fat Bastard Gourmet Billy B Damned
1 tbsp hot sauce (I used Psycho Juice Smoked Ghost Pepper)
Loaf of bread
Coleslaw, pickled Jalapeños, and grated mature cheddar, to serve

Method

1. Pre-heat your oven to 250°F (120°C)

2. Combine the paprika, oregano, cumin, Cayenne, salt, and black pepper.

3. Rub the pork with half the olive oil and massage the spice mixture into your meat.

4. Get a large pan smoking hot and seal your pork on all sides.

5. Put your pork in the oven and cook for around 5 hours or until the meat is fall-apart tender.

6. Remove the fat from the pork and shred the meat using a couple of forks.

7. Put the BBQ sauce in a pan and add the Psycho Juice, followed by the pulled pork, and heat gently until the meat is coated and nice and hot.

8. Cut your bread into slices, lightly toast, and stuff with the pulled pork. Top the meat with coleslaw, pickled Jalapeños, and a sprinkling of cheese if you fancy it.

Psycho Jerk Chicken

There are some fantastic jerk sauces, pastes, and seasonings around, so feel free to use a shop-bought one if you haven't got the time to make your own, but if you fancy making it from scratch, with a Psycho twist, give this one a bash.

INGREDIENTS (Serves 4)

4 chicken legs, skin on

For the jerk paste:

4 Scotch Bonnet peppers, chopped
4 garlic cloves, chopped
1 onion, chopped
4 scallions (spring onions), chopped
1 tsp allspice berries
1 tsp thyme
½ tsp nutmeg
1 tsp black pepper
½ tsp salt
1 tbsp Ghost Pepper hot sauce (I used Psycho Juice 70%)
3 tbsp dark soy sauce
3 tbsp white wine vinegar
3 tbsp vegetable oil
Juice of half a lime

Method

1. First job is to make your jerk paste. Whack all the ingredients (not the chicken) into a food-processor and give it a good old blitz until you get a nice consistency.

2. Score the chicken legs to make slits in the flesh, put them in a bowl, and add about two thirds of the jerk paste. Work the paste thoroughly into the chicken with your hands.

3. Cover the bowl and bang it into the fridge to marinate for at least 2 hours, but preferably overnight. The longer you leave it, then the more jerk flavor it will absorb.

4. Remove the chicken from the bowl and discard the jerk paste.

5. For the best results cook on a BBQ that's good and hot. Start chicken off over the hottest part of the BBQ to get some color on it and then cook for about 15–20 minutes over a lower heat. Brush the chicken with the remaining jerk paste as it cooks to give it even more jerk goodness.

6. Alternatively, pre-heat your oven to 400°F (200°C) and cook the chicken in a roasting tray for about 40 minutes. Turn the chicken halfway through cooking and brush with remaining jerk paste.

Psycho Wings

INGREDIENTS (Serves 4-6)

Regular Hot
4½ lb (2 kg) chicken wings
5 oz (150ml) Habanero hot sauce (I used Psycho Juice 70%)
½ cup (125 g) melted butter

Extra Hot
4½ lb (2 kg) chicken wings
5 oz (150 ml) Red Savina hot sauce (I used Psycho Juice 70%)
½ cup (125 g) melted butter

Caribbean-Style Extra Hot
4½ lb (2 kg) chicken wings
5 oz (150 ml) hot sauce (I used Psycho Juice Mustard Ghost Pepper)
½ cup (125 g) melted butter

Crazy Hot
4½ lb (2 kg) chicken wings
5 oz (150 ml) Ghost Pepper hot sauce (I used Psycho Juice 70%)
½ cup (125 g) melted butter

Take Your Face Off Hot
4½ lb (2 kg) chicken wings
5 oz (150 ml) Ghost Pepper hot sauce (I used Psycho Juice 70%)
1 tsp Psycho Juice Extreme Ghost Pepper hot sauce
½ cup (125 g) melted butter

Smokey-Style Extra Hot
4½ lb (2 kg) chicken wings
5 oz (150 ml) smoked hot sauce (I used Psycho Juice Smoked Ghost Pepper hot sauce
½ cup (125 g) melted butter

Method

1. Either deep fry the wings in batches at 375°F (190°C) for around 8 minutes or oven roast them for around 30 minutes at 390°F (200°C). Your shout. Just make sure they're nice and golden.

2. Gently melt the butter in a saucepan over a low heat, or in 10-second bursts in the microwave.

3. Combine the hot sauce of your choice with the melted butter in a bowl and mix well.

4. Chuck your cooked chicken wings into the sauce and toss until they are fully coated and serve straight away.

I sell some great wing sauces which are good to go straight out of the bottle, but for a brilliant alternative try melting some butter into one of my own Psycho Juice hot sauces. The result is a fantastic wing sauce that coats the chicken really well and it makes such a difference to the flavor when you use real butter. Don't forget to get those wings good and crispy.

Chili Beef & Chorizo Psycho Pizza

INGREDIENTS (Serves 1-2)

3 tbsp olive oil
1 red onion, finely chopped
2 garlic cloves, crushed
1 red bell pepper, finely chopped
4 fresh red chilies, finely chopped
8 oz (225 g) ground (minced) beef
3½ oz (100 g) chorizo, thinly sliced
1 tbsp smoked hot sauce (I used Psycho Juice Smoked Ghost Pepper)
2 tsp paprika
2 tsp ground cumin
1 tsp Mexican oregano
1 tsp ground coriander
½ cup (125g) canned red kidney beans, drained
1 tbsp Red Savina hot sauce (I used Psycho Juice 70%)
1¼ cups (300 ml) tomato sauce for pasta
12 in. (30 cm) pizza base (feel free to make your own but it's a lot less messing about if you just buy one)
¾ cup (90 g) mozzarella, grated
¾ cup (90 g) mature cheddar, grated
Salt and black pepper

I've always thought that pizza is pretty much the perfect vehicle for hot sauce. Just a slice of simple cheese and tomato pizza with a liberal dose of my Psycho Juice 70% Red Savina hot sauce splashed on top is heaven. This recipe has the chili firepower within its ingredients so, if you need to tone it down, just add less.

Method

1. If you've decided to make your own pizza base, then you'd better get started. Whilst you're sifting and kneading and rolling and resting and proving and generally messing about getting flour all over the place, the rest of us will crack on.

2. Heat the olive oil in a frying pan and add the onion, garlic, red pepper, and chilies. Gently fry until nicely softened.

3. Crank the heat up and add the ground beef and chorizo. Get it well colored. Add the hot sauce and keep stirring. It might make you cough a bit. Man up.

4. Chuck in a sprinkle of salt and black pepper, and add the paprika, cumin, oregano, and coriander. Keep cooking and stirring for about 10 minutes. Add the red kidney beans and cook for a further 5 minutes.

5. Mix the Psycho Juice 70% Red Savina hot sauce into the tomato sauce and spread over your pizza base (unless you're still messing around making it).

6. Spoon the beef-and-chorizo mixture on top of the tomato sauce and top with the grated mozzarella and mature cheddar.

7. Cook your pizza in a pre-heated oven at about 430°F (220°C) for 15–20 minutes until nice and crisp and golden.

Index

Acknowledgments

Despite the fact that I wrote every bloody word of this book myself th
are a few people that I'd like to thank.

My mum for fucking off when I was a nipper. Probably better that way
before I got to know you.

My dad for not fucking off when I was a nipper and even sticking by m
when my life went so far off the rails it ended up in a total blood
train wreck.

Jack Daniel's and Thatchers Cider for all the good times. Although yo
are no longer part of my life the memories remain. Well, some of the
I still miss you.

Raymond Vahan Damadian for inventing the MRI Scanner that discovered t
damage to my brain before it was too late. Unfortunately this led to
having to part company with my friends above which was a real shame

Motörhead, the hardest working, dirtiest, filthiest rock 'n' roll band
the world for providing the soundtrack to my life and Lemmy in
particular for doing it his way with a complete no-bullshit attitud
100% genuine legend and the closest thing I ever found to religion.

Emily and Leo for running the shop while I was away writing the book.
Neither of you know how to empty the bin, but you did a great job.

Steve Bright, artistic genius and official portrait painter to
Dr. Burnorium. You can't judge a book by its cover but I'm proud t
have Steve's work on the front of mine.

Luther, Chip, Sandy, and Kris, my US friends who helped make my dream
open the UK's first hot shop a reality. Working with you is a blast

Paul Grant and Duane Shield for dealing with all the financial
bureaucratic business bullshit and for also proving that not all
accountants are tedious, boring fuckers.

Pete Jorgensen, my editor who embraced the madness as I wrote it and
laughed in the right places. It's been great fun. I reserve the right
replace my thanks with scathing criticism depending on the final edit
still can't believe you spoilt my joke by not letting me say c***.

Phil Bawn, a true friend with a wicked sense of humour. Very crafty, b
definitely one in a million. One hand mate.

Lauren, Blaine, Ellie, and Liam for being such great kids despite havi
me as a dad. You're all far more mature than I am and I love you dear

Lisa, my long-suffering wife. Where or what would I be without you?
Fucking hell. It doesn't bear thinking about. Allowing you to chat
up is still the best thing I've ever done in my life. Thanks for
loving me, thanks for believing in me, and thanks for being the bes
mum in the world to our kids. You keep all this crazy shit together

About the Author

Dr. Burnorium has almost 20 years of experience sampling, selling, and spreading the word about the world's finest—and hottest—sauces. He's currently based in Bristol, England where he educates ~~victims~~ customers in the ways of ass-blasting heat. Visit his websites at hotsauceemporium.co.uk and psychojuice.com